1978

The Emergence of the Latin American Novel

FOR GISELA LANGSDORFF

THE EMERGENCE OF
the Latin American novel

GORDON BROTHERSTON

Reader in Literature, University of Essex

CAMBRIDGE UNIVERSITY PRESS

CAMBRIDGE

LONDON · NEW YORK · MELBOURNE

Published by the Syndics of the Cambridge University Press
The Pitt Building, Trumpington Street, Cambridge CB2 1RP
Bentley House, 200 Euston Road, London NW1 2DB
32 East 57th Street, New York, NY 10022, USA
296 Beaconsfield Parade, Middle Park, Melbourne 3206, Australia

First published 1977

Printed in Great Britain by
Western Printing Services Ltd, Bristol

Library of Congress cataloguing in publication data

Brotherston, Gordon.
The emergence of the Latin American novel.
Bibliography: p.
Includes index.
1. Spanish American fiction – 20th century – History
and criticism. I. Title.
PQ7082.N7B66   863'.03   76–40834
ISBN 0 521 21478 5

CONTENTS

PREFACE

This book is meant as an introduction to the Latin American novel, especially to writers of the last three decades. It is offered as a scholarly work which nonetheless is accessible to the reader with little or no knowledge of Spanish (or Portuguese). I am grateful to several people for the help they have given me in the preparation of this book over the last three years: Michael Black, Robert Clark, Jürgen Golte, Peter Hulme, Robert Pring-Mill and Arthur Terry; a group of students at the University of British Columbia, Robert Demaine, John Kirk, Tim O'Connor, Meredyth Savage and Margarita Sewerin; Pat Marsden for compiling the index; and my wife, to whom the final result is dedicated. Details of works mentioned in the text or specified by a translated title are given in the bibliography; translations are mine unless otherwise stated. Passages in some chapters have been reworked from articles of mine in *Comparative Literature Studies, Hispania, Romance Notes, Style* and *The Times Literary Supplement.*

Acknowledgement is made for permission to quote and translate copyright material: M. A. Asturias, from *Hombres de maíz*, Editorial Losada S.A.; and from *El señor presidente*, English translation *The President* by F. Partridge, by permission of V. Gollancz Ltd.; A. Carpentier, from *El siglo de las luces*, English translation *Explosion in a Cathedral* by J. Sturrock, by permission of V. Gollancz Ltd.; J. C. Onetti, from *Juntacadáveres*, Revista de Occidente S.A.; J. Rulfo, from *Pedro Páramo*, Fondo de cultura económica; J. Cortázar, from *Rayuela*, English translation *Hopscotch* by G. Rabassa, by permission of Pantheon Books/A Division of Random House Inc., Copyright © Random House, New York, N.Y., 1966; J. M. Arguedas, from *El zorro de arriba y el zorro de abajo*, Editorial Losada S.A.; M. Vargas Llosa, from *La ciudad y los perros*, English translation *The Time of the Hero* by L. Kemp, by permission of Grove Press and Jonathan Cape

Ltd.; G. García Márquez, from *Cien años de soledad,* English translation *One Hundred Years of Solitude* by G. Rabassa, by permission of Harper and Rowe Publishers Inc. and Jonathan Cape Ltd.

G.B.

Wivenhoe, May 1973 –
Vancouver, November 1975

The novel of Latin America (Spanish America and Brazil) has not long existed as a definable entity. That it does now is due above all to a number of modern writers who, in their novels and criticism, have created a literary tradition which transcends the boundaries of their separate nations and regions. Among them are those made famous by translation and acclaim abroad: the Nobel prize-winner Miguel Ángel Asturias, Alejo Carpentier (whose work has been published in 14 languages), Carlos Fuentes, Mario Vargas Llosa, Gabriel García Márquez, Julio Cortázar; and those less widely known: Juan Carlos Onetti, José Donoso, Juan Rulfo, João Guimarães Rosa, José María Arguedas. These and other writers have achieved for the novel, as a genre, what the Modernists did for poetry, at the turn of the century in Spanish America, and in the 1920s in Brazil.[1] In this, as in any other case, 'tradition' means recourse to precedent, however close in time. In the 1930s the Peruvian Luis Alberto Sánchez could say, polemically, that the Latin American novel didn't exist.[2] And he was right, not because no-one in that area had ever published a novel, but in so far as common points of reference, a literary context, were hard to discern. Few novelists had even attempted to explore the complexities of their own environment. Since then, in the last three decades, there have appeared novels which 'take on' Latin America as their formal subject – *The Lost Steps* (*Los pasos perdidos*, 1953) by Carpentier, *One Hundred Years of Solitude* (*Cien años de soledad*, 1967), *The Autumn of the Patriarch* (*El otoño del patriarca*, 1975) by García Márquez, *The Fox from Above and the Fox from Below* (*El zorro de arriba y el zorro de abajo*, 1971) by Arguedas, *Manuel's Book* (*Libro de Manuel*, 1973) by Cortázar – and also a body of critical interpretation, matters about which at least to disagree. This new general awareness is manifest in critical studies by the novelists themselves, such as Vargas Llosa's commentaries on Arguedas and García Márquez, Edmundo Desnoes's pungent essay on Carpentier, Fuentes's survey *The New Latin American Novel* (*La nueva novela hispanoamericana*, 1969), and Donoso's personal history of the 'boom' of the novel in the 1960s.[3] And this 'consensus' (to use Sánchez's word) has stimulated the very process of literary creation.

There is no single reason for this recent flowering of the Latin American novel. The political, social and racial diversity which has characterized the various states of the subcontinent since the independence movements of the early nineteenth century remains as formidable as ever. And a developed sense of historical community is hardly more accessible now than it was to those pioneers of the novel who vainly aspired to imitate the realists of post-Revolutionary France. Still, in this century the global realignments after the Second World War gave the term Latin America a new political significance. And numerous internal movements towards greater emancipation, so often crushed (as in Bolivia, Brazil, Nicaragua) but triumphant, at least for a time, in Mexico and then in Cuba in 1959, have provided a thread of inner coherence akin to that which linked the novelists of nineteenth-century Russia, from Lermontov and Gogol to Tolstoi and Gorki.

As the forlorn 'vanguard' of Latin America, an actual example of the revolutionary theory elaborated by Che Guevara, Régis Debray and others, Cuba no doubt merits a volume to itself. Castro's famous 'Words to the Intellectuals' had a profound effect on Latin American writers: a message very different from Stalin's socialist realism, for they placed hope in the creativity of socialist man rather than political regimentation.[4] Endeavours to embody the positive ideals of the state are visible in the work of Onelio Jorge Cardoso, Manuel Cofiño, Lisandro Otero, Guillermo Cabrera Infante (who later, however, in *Three Trapped Tigers*, *Tres tristes tigres*, 1967, changed his politics and his style), Alejo Carpentier (who sacrificed much of his previous subtlety in the process),[5] Edmundo Desnoes, in his magnificent *Memories of Underdevelopment* (*Memorias del subdesarrollo*, 1967); and, outside Cuba, the Bolivian Renato Prada and the Uruguayans Mario Benedetti and Carlos Martínez Moreno. Yet the remarkable José Lezama Lima, a professed Roman Catholic, has not let the revolution directly affect his novels, while others have if anything been critical of it – Reinaldo Arenas, for example, in his novel *Hallucinations (El mundo alucinante,* 1967). Moreover, at least in the first years of its existence, revolutionary Cuba had a more widespread and fertile influence as an intellectual centre, a common meeting ground, of the kind that Mexico was in the 1920s and which otherwise has been provided by such foreign cities as Paris and Barcelona. The Peruvian Vargas Llosa and the (then) Argentinian Cortázar visited Havana more than once and for several years served as editors of the review *Casa de las Américas,* which became a continental critical forum for the new novelists;[6] the Colombian García Márquez worked for the Cuban news agency Prensa Latina, and, with many others, the Peruvian Arguedas has served on the panels which award the annual literary prizes of the *Casa de las Américas* and the Writers' Union.

In other words, an undeniable factor in the 'rise of the novel' in Latin America has been a reciprocal self-awareness among novelists in different countries and in which Cuba has been instrumental. This consciousness is comparable with that shared in very different political circumstances, by the novelists of eighteenth-century England. How important this kind of communication has been is shown by the 'continental' novels mentioned above, and towards which this study is directed. The concern inevitably means that I pass over many notable novelists, among them Eduardo Mallea, Ernesto Sábato, Eduardo Barrios, whose metaphysical and other concerns have diverged from those of their contemporaries. Nonetheless, to approach the Latin American novel thus, from the inside, is to offer a means of discussing a subject that has proved notoriously difficult to focus on, from the time that Latin America began to exist.[7]

My first chapter situates the modern novel retrospectively, since, as Borges has remarked, writers create (even if they don't always acknowledge) their own precursors. There is nothing sacred about the number (8) of novelists examined in detail (they could have included for example, Guimarães Rosa, Fuentes, Donoso), nor about the order in which they are taken (the date of their first important work). Each comes from a different national and geographical situation in Latin America, from the cities of the River Plate to provincial Mexico, from the Quechua-speaking

Andes and the Maya forests of Central America to the historically complex Caribbean. And each shares the continental consciousness I have mentioned, as a contributor to the 'rise' of the novel in the last three decades. I have not concentrated on any one modern Brazilian novelist largely because of the barrier which continues to exist between the Portuguese and Spanish languages in Latin America, despite, for example, the profound effect of the work of João Guimarães Rosa on José María Arguedas.

Each of the eight chapters dedicated to these eight novelists opens with a long quotation from his work. Starting with so close a focus may seem precipitate; and in principle excerpts from novels are likely to be unrepresentative. But few studies of the modern Latin American novel offer practical criticism of the kind I attempt. The quotations are meant to be substantial enough to show how the novelist in question writes, so that discussion may refer to something visible on the page. Though the emphasis is textual in this sense, the commentaries are not confined to style, narrowly understood, but are shaped by the overall considerations raised in the first chapter and returned to in the last.

1   Settings and people

Two of the first major prose works of independent Latin America were not conventional novels at all: *Facundo. Civilization and Barbarism (Civilización y barbarie*, 1845), by the Argentinian D. F. Sarmiento, and *Rebellion in the Backlands (Os sertões*, 1902), by the Brazilian Euclides da Cunha. They remain fundamental because of the way they bring together, on a grand scale, elements of the most diverse and intractable order, in their literary exploration of the Latin American environment.

In both books we move from the civilization of the coast and the political capital (Buenos Aires; Rio de Janeiro) towards the hinterland and the dark 'interior' of the sub-continent. From the familiar streets and the bourgeois constitutions of cities of European origin we are removed to the 'realms unknown', the 'worlds of solitude' beyond, to quote phrases applied to South America by the English poet James Thomson in *The Seasons*.[1] In this unknown world the new arrival encounters strange and often forbidding landscapes, and people no less strange and forbidding, whose ways of life proved incompatible with that of the city.

The very title of Sarmiento's book announces the importance of this incompatibility, and what Sarmiento himself thinks of the 'barbarians' outside the city gates. *Facundo* has, in fact, an ideological message and was directed against an historical figure, the Argentinian general Juan Facundo Quiroga, known as the 'Tiger of the Plains'. Like the more famous Rosas, dictator of the Argentine from 1829 to 1853, Facundo was implacably opposed to the enlightened ideas of progress which Sarmiento put into practice as best he could when he became liberal president of the country in 1868. By origin Facundo was a gaucho, a cowboy of the pampas, who held the life of the city and its customs in contempt. In order to explain this hostility Sarmiento stresses the role of environment in the formation of social and political attitudes and presents

Facundo as the product of a world he believed to be destructive by inclination and unable to help itself.

Sarmiento's great emphasis is on the city as the indispensable focus of civilized life:

> All civilization, whether native, Spanish, or European, centres in the cities, where are to be found the manufactories, the shops, the schools and colleges, and other characteristics of civilized nations. Elegance of style, articles of luxury, dress-coats, and frock-coats, with other European garments, occupy their appropriate place in these towns. I mention these small matters designedly. It is sometimes the case that the only city of a pastoral province is its capital, and occasionally the land is uncultivated up to its very streets. The encircling desert besets such cities at a greater or less distance, and bears heavily upon them, and they are thus small oases of civilization surrounded by an untilled plain, hundreds of square miles in extent, the surface of which is but rarely interrupted by any settlement of consequence.[2]

In this polarized situation, even such 'small matters' as style of dress acquire enormous significance:

> The inhabitants of the city wear the European dress, live in a civilized manner, and possess laws, ideas of progress, means of instruction, some municipal organization, regular forms of government, etc. Beyond the precincts of the city everything assumes a new aspect; the country people wear a different dress, which I will call South American, as it is common to all districts; their habits of life are different, their wants peculiar and limited. The people composing these two distinct forms of society, do not seem to belong to the same nation. Moreover, the countryman, far from attempting to imitate the customs of the city, rejects with disdain its luxury and refinement; and it is unsafe for the costume of the city people, their coats, their cloaks, their saddles, or anything European, to show themselves in the country. Everything civilized which the city contains is blockaded there, proscribed beyond its limits; and any one who should

dare to appear in the rural districts in a frock-coat, for
example, or mounted on an English saddle, would bring
ridicule and brutal assaults upon himself.

Yet more brutal are the assaults of the 'savages' roaming the
'uncertain horizon' of this untilled land, the untamed Indians who
raid by night like beasts of prey. The world outside the civilized
oasis is not without its 'poetry' and its magic. But it is backward
and dangerous, the cradle of men like the barbarous Facundo,
and in mortal conflict with the progress championed by Sarmiento.

In *Facundo*, Sarmiento's purpose is clearly didactic and propa-
gandist, and he does his best to denigrate and ridicule his ideological opponent. Yet as if conscious of the vulnerability of his own
position as a Europeanized intellectual, he does not deprive the
'South American' Facundo of all dignity or local power. There is
a similar ambivalence in da Cunha's *Rebellion in the Backlands*,
notable because the Brazilian was more of an evolutionary
Positivist than Sarmiento. The rebellion da Cunha describes, in
the thorny and arid area of Brazil's North East known as the *sertão*,
is 'explained' yet more fundamentally in terms of environment,
and of race. Victims of 'collective psychosis', a certain Antônio
Conselheiro and his followers found in their *terra ignota* a kind
of monstrous anti-city, a cursed Jerusalem, and will not yield to
the laws of the Brazilian nation. Conselheiro is said to be a 'living
document of atavism', one of the worse consequences of his desert
landscape and of admixture with Indian and other 'inferior' races.
Yet he and his followers, with their guerrilla tactics, show great
physical and moral resilience during the long campaigns against
them. And they choose to die sooner than surrender to the government troops (among them, da Cunha). Like Facundo, Conselheiro
forces admiration as a creature more at one with his immediate
environment than his enemies, the representatives of the national
constitution.

Facundo and *Rebellion in the Backlands* both combine report-
age, historical and geographical essay, political tract and embryonic novel, and deserve the epithet 'epic'. They cannot resolve
the conflicts they raise: on the contrary, these reappear continuously in Latin American prose. They disclose incompati-
bilities, in geography, culture and race, which are tragic in so

far as the thriving of one force must mean the extinction of the other.

2

In describing the conflicts inherent in their Latin American environment, Sarmiento and da Cunha gave a much more consistent and realistic account of the world they themselves were at home in than of the one outside it. For them it was hard to focus dispassionately on the realms which bred such men as Facundo and Conselheiro. We are never really shown the communities these alien creatures inhabit from the inside. For all Sarmiento and da Cunha's 'objectivity', uncivilized Latin America remains the source of myths which are often conflicting or self-contradictory. This preferential focus on the city is more pronounced in the novel proper in the nineteenth century when realist writing dealt almost exclusively with civilized life. Indeed the characters and plots of the first realist novels of Latin America appear to rely on the actual physical arrangements of the city, with its streets, interiors, schools, postal service, transport, newspapers, publishing houses, parliamentary debate, police force, sartorial fashions and banks, and the whole mental world these things imply. *Amalia* (1851), a novel by Sarmiento's compatriot José Mármol, well illustrates this relationship between physical and literary form. The codes and conventions of Buenos Aires, the dress and even the speech of the place, which are the substance of the novel, are threatened and destroyed by the 'barbaric' Rosas, as he strengthens his dictatorial power in the capital. Within the novel itself we move from realism to myth and melodrama, and to open diatribe against the iniquities of Rosas. Faced with this phenomenon we are not surprised to discover that the few successful realist authors of nineteenth-century Latin America came from cities notable for their constitutional stability, above all Santiago de Chile (the refuge of Sarmiento in exile and the adoptive home of the great reformer and educationalist Andrés Bello), and Rio de Janeiro. As settings appropriate to the themes of Balzac and the European realists, these places appear indispensable in the novels of Alberto Blest Gana and Joaquim Machado de Assis.

In Blest Gana's novels, the society of the Chilean capital appears finely stratified by class (old aristocracy, new-rich capitalist, aspirant lower middle class, and so on), with still finer sub-categories (within the servant class, for example). We are presented with a true *comédie humaine*, which can be enacted since hierarchy and role are not rigidly identified with 'character'. In this respect *Martín Rivas* (1862), a 'novel of political and social customs', is exemplary. In 1850, a time of constitutional crisis and tension between conservatives and egalitarian liberals in Chile, the hero Rivas arrives from the provinces, like one of Balzac's young heroes, or Stendhal's, and 'makes good' in the capital. The story is a long one, and here we need only note the degree to which Blest Gana relies on notions of social contract and exchange within the city, into which Rivas is drawn in a way that Sarmiento's 'South Americans' refused to be. Blest Gana is remarkable for the degree to which he makes the city the centre of attraction and the model of organization and taste. Nuances of social intercourse are superbly caught: for instance, the beautiful upper-class Leonor is made uncertain by Rivas's awkward show of being offended by her, but recognizes that she wouldn't have thought twice about the matter had another of her class, and not Rivas, been involved. With his whiff of Rousseau's natural man, as yet unspoilt by society and civilized conventions, the provincial Rivas does not triumph as a self-reliant pioneer, but as one who learns how to strengthen the bourgeois structure.[3] This means marrying Leonor and into her rich family, forgetting revolutionary politics and unnaturally (in Rousseau's terms) flaunting success before one's country cousins. From his own superior position in civilized society, Blest Gana endeavours to foster its growth, by making such a man as Martín Rivas a 'model worthy of imitation'.

To this extent Blest Gana identified himself more with Santiago than Machado de Assis did with Rio de Janeiro. After uncertain literary beginnings as romancer and poet of the American wilds, Machado de Assis restricted himself to describing life in the civilized enclave from which da Cunha's expeditionary force had been ordered out. The novels he produced as a result are masterly by any standards: *Posthumous memoirs of Bras Cubas* (*Memorias posthumas de Bras Cubas*, 1880), *Quincas Borba* (1892) and *Dom Casmurro* (1900).[4] Like Blest Gana, Machado de Assis relied technically on the actual structure of the city, though he committed himself far less overtly to the defence of the bourgeoisie. Indeed his detachment and irony lend him an unexpected modernity, and he is comparable to Borges in the way he exposes the underlying fallacies of realist fiction. The self-critical and reflexive nature of his novels, moreover, has led some critics to regard him as an essentially post-realist writer. There is perhaps some truth in this view; at the same time we should note that the first of the mature novels, the 'posthumous memoirs' of an ostensibly dead and treacherously self-deprecating first-person narrator (Bras Cubas) is far more 'sophisticated' in this sense than the later ones.

A reason for this apparent anomaly is indicated by Machado de Assis himself in his prologue to the *Posthumous memoirs*, where he speaks of his fondness for Lawrence Sterne and Xavier de Maistre. These were 'conversational' writers for whom *how* to approach a notional subject mattered more than narrative descriptions in the style of their realist contemporaries. Machado de Assis was chary of approaching bourgeois Rio as a subject because of his ambiguous feelings towards its inhabitants, and towards his very success as a man of letters ('God alone knows the power of an adjective, especially in new, tropical countries'). The child of a mulatto in a state where slavery was not abolished until 1888, he rose socially because of his literary talent. Like the first-person narrator Bras Cubas, he was both fascinated by and detached from the life surrounding him. The depth of his ambivalence is well caught in the pleasurable yet 'absurd' affair Bras has with the beautiful bourgeoise Virgilia, a far more complex relationship than Martín Rivas's with Leonor in Blest Gana's book. He is deeply sceptical of civilized values yet sees no alternative to them. At one point he thinks of 'running away' with Virgilia to start a new life 'in the country' or in distant Europe: 'with the world, morality, and her husband all eliminated we would share our house with no one but the angels'. But the idea is immediately shown to be romantic and futile, and they settle for a 'little secluded house with a garden, on some out-of-the-way street'. The aimless Bras-ilian hero stays on in an environment that is indispensable but insubstantial and unreal. We are faced, then, with the striking fact that the greatest novelist of nineteenth-century Latin America presented the city life of his time in a way which gently but completely undermined the bases of its existence.

This tendency becomes more specific in the 'Buenos Aires' novels of Eugenio Cambaceres. The most important of these, *Drifting* (*Sin rumbo*, 1885) has as its hero Andrés, a member of the landowning elite, who is satisfied neither by the 'natural' life on his estate nor by the sophistication of the capital. He scorns those who have any sense of national responsibility: as with José Mármol, the realist convention of the novel is broken by direct political comment, this time on Sarmiento's presidential policies. Yet Andrés's experience of Buenos Aires, and hence the reader's, is confined to the world of the Italian opera and the theatre, and his own *garçonière*, modelled on the decadent interiors of Des Esseintes, in J.-K. Huysmans's *À Rebours*. It is as if, through his protagonist, Cambaceres would or could not find a better or more solid life in Buenos Aires to be involved in, remaining 'superior' in so far as he is exquisitely imbued with European taste. But perhaps Andrés is really inferior, in so far as he is made to seem exemplary too, as an anti-hero, a useless citizen, the victim, like Paul Bourget's *Le Disciple*, of unconstructive nineteenth-century ideas (overdoses of Schopenhauer and the Decadents). Cambaceres's emphasis is less social and political than Blest Gana's or Machado de Assis's, and more philosophical, or even medical, oppressively so in the 'case-history' prose of the later chapters. Nonetheless, before Andrés goes back to the pampa to die (in a scene which blends sentimentality with Naturalism), he wakens to hidden forces in his land that are far stronger than anything he himself represents. These stem from the dark recesses of 'revolutionary' Argentina and threaten not just the decadent but the whole bourgeois system. In this, Cambaceres anticipates the dilemmas of later writers like Ricardo Güiraldes, or Eduardo Mallea, and even of Borges, and Cortázar (who mentions Cambaceres in his own novels).

The 'small oases of civilization' of European origin, which Sarmiento did his best to defend in Latin America, also provided subject matter for the first realist novels in that part of the world. Yet already in these early novels we may detect a sense of the precariousness of this subject matter. With his exemplary hero, Blest Gana set out deliberately to strengthen the bourgeois

structure, as if conscious of some weakness in it; and in their different ways Machado de Assis and Cambaceres cast doubts on its enduring viability in the larger geographical and political context of
Latin America.

3

The connection between the nineteenth- and the twentieth-century
urban novel in Latin America is long and intricate. In some cases
it is easy enough to perceive. Blest Gana's bourgeoisie lives on,
for example, in the novels of José Donoso and other Chileans,[5]
in a changed role perhaps, but as recognizably the same social
group. More often the connection can be made only by
reconstructing the huge social and political changes of twentieth-
century Latin American history, the violent proletarian movements, for example, which Manuel Rojas described in such a
way as to make him (in the opinion of Jean Franco)[6] 'the major
realist writer of Latin America'. For our purposes the main point
is the radical uncertainty about the role of the city, which we
found in the very origins of the realist novel. With Juan Carlos
Onetti this uncertainty was exacerbated to an extreme degree. His
account of Buenos Aires in the 1930s, which has been hailed as
'the first modern novel of Latin America' (Emir Rodríguez
Monegal), is significantly entitled *No Man's Land* (*Tierra de nadie*,
1941); and subsequent urban novels of his have a setting, Santa
Maria, which is repeatedly shown to be virtual and imaginary.
As if searching for some palpable, tangible social reality Onetti
concentrates on the life of the deprived and the outlawed; and
as a common meeting-ground for his characters he chooses the
brothel, the 'lowest' product of city life. This modern counter-
part of the half-illicit, half-folk gatherings in the houses of
the aspirant lower middle class (*gente de medio pelo*), which
served as the only venue for all social classes in *Martín Rivas*,
has the same basic function in the work of a surprising number
of other modern novelists (among them, Vargas Llosa, García
Márquez, Fuentes and José María Arguedas). Furthermore this
persistent lack of confidence in Latin American 'oases of civilization' has gone hand in hand with the gradual exploration of the
world outside, as an alternative 'home'. The epic achievement

of Carpentier or Asturias can best be appreciated in this perspective.

It was not until the appearance of certain pivotal novels in the 1920s and 1930s, by Rómulo Gallegos, Ricardo Güiraldes and José Eustacio Rivera, that the traditional conflict between 'civilization and barbarism' was restated with growing interest in the latter term. Before this date we may note Jorge Isaacs's 'American' novel *María* (1867), if only because it was once the most read novel of Latin America (it is barely readable today). Isaacs's story unfolds against the magnificent scenery of the Cauca valley in Colombia. But this piece of the American wilds is no more than scenery and to all intents and purposes uninhabited. It is a theatrical backdrop, with just the right ingredients of the luscious and the sublime, for the bourgeois furnishings and interiors which make up the world of the main characters. Unlike Isaacs, Gallegos, Güiraldes and Rivera send their characters out of town to live among other populations: the cowboys of the Venezuelan plains, the gauchos, or the rubber-tappers of the Amazon jungle. The fascination of this 'other' life outside the city is now fully acknowledged, though it still remains incompatible with the novelists' 'real' world. The fundamental importance, in Latin American literary history, of these three exploratory novelists has been lucidly stated by Trinidad Pérez (1971) and other critics.

For Gallegos (who like Sarmiento became a liberal president of his country) matters are relatively simple. When the conflicts between his obviously allegorical characters come to a head, the code of the land has to yield to that of the city. Our excursions into the countryside and its folklore are pleasant enough; and we are even alerted to the sinister effect of U.S. capital on 'underdeveloped' Latin America. Above all, as an emblem of rural Venezuela, 'Doña Bárbara', in the novel named after her (1929), is a distinctly more alluring creature than Facundo. She is also shown to have been wronged, exploited and misunderstood. Nonetheless her power is curtailed, and in the end she succumbs to her enlightened opponent from Caracas, Santos Luzardo.

Setting and character in Güiraldes's famous picture of gaucho life, *Don Segundo Sombra* (1926), are less schematic and less obviously dualistic than they are in *Doña Bárbara*. Endowed with the shadowy quality of his name, Don Segundo successfully eludes moral analysis as the mentor of the young lad who tells the story. An apparent orphan, his pupil crosses a bridge to a fuller life among the gauchos, and there learns to 'be a man', very much like the boy brought up by the Cape Cod fishermen in Kipling's *Captains Courageous* (Waldo Frank was sooner reminded of Huckleberry Finn). However, when his true birthright is discovered and he comes of age, the lad is recalled and sent back to Buenos Aires. 'Real life' turns out to be in the city after all, and not out there in the backlands. Güiraldes is more subtle than Gallegos; but this may be because his gauchos had become a vanishing breed in Argentina. His elegiac treatment of these old enemies of progress recalls that of the Modernists who influenced him, notably Rubén Darío who in the 1890s wrote a valedictory poem ('Del campo') to the gaucho from Buenos Aires, the city he called 'cosmopolis'.

The fate of the explorer in Rivera's *The Vortex* (*La vorágine*, 1924) is, by comparison, extreme. Having left the capital city (Bogotá), Arturo Cova strays out over the vast plains of northern South America, drawn as if fatefully to their further edge, the uncertain horizon[7] where yet more savage wilds begin. And he enters the 'green mansions' of the jungle (to use the title of one of W. H. Hudson's South American romances), whose power of attraction he cannot now escape. This environment disintegrates him, with its mind-destroying life cycles, oppressive vegetation, snakes, piranhas and human savages. Cova tells his story in the first person, and as the vortex claims him, his old points of reference, and then his sanity itself, forsake him. The prose of the narrative is affected by what it describes, and demonstrates why it cannot go on in such a situation. The last news Rivera, as 'editor' of his papers, gives us of Cova, is that the jungle devoured him. Fearsome and destructive, as an extreme form of the American wilds, the jungle is shown nonetheless to have a life and a majestic self-sufficiency of its own: it is not merely antithetical to the city. Its 'cosmic force' emanates from hidden depths, where 'unknown gods speak in half-tones' and immemorial trees have witnessed the presence of primeval tribes. It is a vegetable universe, a solitary family with its own solidarity, which (in Rivera's striking phrase) 'never betrays itself'. Rivera's novel is uneven, but is remarkable as a thorough-going attempt to register experience beyond the pale of civilization in Latin America. As a first-person narrator who provides a link between antithetical geographical and cultural extremes, and who effectively goes back in time, from the modern city to the cyclic existence of primeval jungle life, Arturo Cova heralds the hero of Carpentier's novel *The Lost Steps* (*Los pasos perdidos*, 1953), the first to attempt to 'synthesize' Latin American experience in the genre. More impressive still, Cova's intuition that the magic forest which claims him, with its ancient trees and strange fauna, may 'incarnate' the mysteries of a whole 'creation' is crucial to the novels of Carpentier, and to Asturias's monumental novel *Men of Maize* (*Hombres de maíz*).

The explorations undertaken separately by these 'regional' novelists, Gallegos, Güiraldes and Rivera, were continued on a continental scale by the Cuban novelist Alejo Carpentier. With Carpentier we enter another phase in the history of the Latin American novel, since he was the first to make his continent his subject. Carpentier's *The Kingdom of this World* (*El reino de este mundo*) and Asturias's *Men of Maize*, both published in 1949, have been called the 'backbone' and the 'inspirational source' of the modern novel.[8] Carpentier paid tribute to the work of Gallegos, Güiraldes and Rivera, and their 'nativism' as explorers in a continent still largely 'unseen' and unknown in literature. But he also endeavoured to distinguish his novels from theirs (and indeed from his own youthful writings) in terms not just of scale, but of 'taste' and attitude. According to him, incarnate in non-European America there was a 'marvellous' reality, which he called 'lo real maravilloso americano', a whole different creation and culture whose chief power was to fascinate. The Latin American novelist should take care to 'name the things' of his New World Eden; and in the process his prose, by its veracity, would acquire a 'magic realism',[9] beside which the old realism of the city and of civilized Europe must pale.

These are notions which Carpentier has worked into his own novels, with shifting emphases. The one which adheres most rigorously to his 'thesis', *The Lost Steps*, reveals most clearly the twin sources of his literary inspiration: the chronicles of the Spanish conquistadors, and the American epic of Chateaubriand, eventually published as *Les Natchez*. The continent is both the scene of fable and an 'innocent' land, exciting to discover, but problematic as a permanent dwelling-place. Carpentier's continental view of America may be said to derive from writers who 'discovered' it from somewhere wholly outside. Unlike them, however, Carpentier is not European, and his main problem as a Latin American novelist has proved to be where to place himself in relation to his 'creation', the paramount problem also for those Latin American poets who have attempted to write an American epic in verse, from Bello, with his 'America', to Neruda's *Canto general*. The very sweep of Carpentier's gesture left him without a foothold; and he resolved the internal oppositions we have been discussing by effectively discounting them. How he, and later 'continental' novelists like García Márquez and Cortázar have dealt with this problem of self-location is discussed in the following chapters.

The objections which critics make to Carpentier's work, as an undeniable point of reference in the Latin American novel, have centred on the claim that he implicitly devalues his own habitat, making it an underdeveloped state. America is magical because it is mythical, pre-social, even pre-rational. The 'indigenous' figures Carpentier enthuses over exist as no more than part of a landscape, there to be enjoyed. Significantly, Carpentier dislikes the 'social' concern of writers like Gallegos. The issue is a complicated one. Nonetheless it is fair to say that Carpentier's novels raise the question: where does the author stand in relation to the America he is describing? Is it really *his* environment and does he have any stake in it?

This elusiveness of Carpentier's sharply distinguishes him from several important near-contemporaries. In the novels of the Brazilian North-East,[10] particularly of the *sertão* first penetrated in prose by da Cunha, and of the provinces of other Latin American countries, notably Mexico, we find a concern with life in the hinterland which gives no glimpse of Carpentier's magic, and depends ultimately on a highly political involvement in the destinies of its inhabitants. The striking similarities between the novels of the Brazilian Graciliano Ramos and the Mexican Juan Rulfo, authors who otherwise have little in common, are best understood in terms of this kind of literary attitude and commitment. This is a commitment which depends on the insight that radical reform movements in Latin America have arisen, not in the cities, as in the classic Marxist hypothesis, but on the land, as in the revolutions which re-shaped Mexico in the first decades of this century and which triumphed in Cuba in 1959. Without these historical developments, characteristic of Latin America, and according to some theorists, of other parts of the 'Third World', the whole-hearted commitment to Castro's Cuba of such 'provincial' writers as Rulfo or José María Arguedas would seem incomprehensible.

4

As a theorist of rural revolution and a champion of the ideological (as well as tactical) importance of the guerrilla 'focus', Régis Debray devoted several pages of his *Revolution in the Revolution?* to the rising against the imperial Spanish led by the Quechua-speaking Tupac Amaru in 1781, in the highlands (sierra) of the Andes. This abortive rebellion by the descendants of the Incas (Tupac Amaru was an ancestral name) preceded the political independence later won by the Spanish-speaking creoles of America (albeit with the help, scantily-acknowledged, of the Quechua and other American Indians).[11] After his defeat Tupac Amaru was tortured and killed by the Spanish in the square at Cuzco, the ancient capital of the Incas. Four horses having failed to pull him apart, his head and limbs were hacked from his body. I mention it not in order to examine Debray's theories (though the political consequences of the failure of guerrilla movements, including Che Guevara's mission, in that same part of South America in the 1960s can hardly be underestimated), but to introduce a yet weightier term of reference into the discussion. That modern novelists otherwise as dissimilar to each other (as we shall see) as the cosmopolitan Cortázar and the provincial Arguedas should show a common respect for Tupac Amaru is eloquent in itself. If the Latin American novel is charged with the exploration of a given environment, then behind such indigenous figures of the hinterland as the gaucho and the sertanejo (as Sarmiento and da Cunha well recognized) stands one far more inaccessible and imposing : the American Indian.[12] Because the basic problem of coming to terms with this yet more 'alien' figure has remained the same, attempts to characterize these prior inhabitants of the continent constitute a remarkably coherent tradition within the Latin American novel,[13] a tradition in which the questions raised so far appear in heightened and more urgent form.

Novels about the American Indian go back well into the nineteenth century, and in origin are inseparable from European Romanticism. The Brazilian 'Americanists' as they called themselves (José de Alencar, Antonio Gonçalves Dias, the young Machado de Assis and others) responded to the fact of Brazilian independence by turning to the 'wild' peoples of their land in the attempt to convert them into a guarantee of cultural separateness from Europe, on a national or even a continental scale. The title of the best known novel of this kind is the name of an Indian maiden and an anagram of America: *Iracema* (1866) by Alencar. The customs and speech of the Indians were to become, it was hoped, a more authentic local source of inspiration, were to provide models for social and political behaviour. While in principle no more or less surprising than the policy by which the framers of the U.S. constitution took note of the laws of the Iroquois Civilized Tribes, in practice this programme did not make much headway, despite the laudable attempts of the Brazilians to get to know surviving Indians and to learn languages like Tupi-Guarani (once the lingua franca of coastal Brazil). The gulf between their bourgeois life in Rio and the largely extinct customs of scattered tribes, was simply too great.

At the same period in Mexico, very different ideals, which nonetheless left Indian culture in an equally marginal position, were embraced by Ignacio Altamirano and by those whom he influenced as reformer and educator. Though he grew up an Aztec, and did not learn Spanish until he went to school, Altamirano devoted all his energy to fostering civilized and Positivist ideals similar to those of Sarmiento, da Cunha and Andrés Bello. His (posthumous) novel *The Zarco* (1901) is one of the most extraordinary products of Latin American literature. Written as an exemplary work, designed to educate the masses, its characters have the obviousness and the power of a cartoon. (Altamirano expressed admiration for the simplified characterization in novels by Dickens and the German-Swiss educator Heinrich Zschokke). The Zarco himself is a bandit. Blue-eyed (*zarco*) and fair-haired, an apt blend of conquistador and Texas gunman, he represents the harmful and destructive forces once foreign to Mexico. Altamirano took him as an example of the bandits who roamed the country in the early 1860s, living off the land and terrorizing the towns. The real hero of the novel, the modest Indian blacksmith Nicolás, is his opposite, and a paragon. But though his skin still denotes his race, in every other respect Nicolás has become a white man, a creature of the Mexican bourgeoisie ('It was acknowledged that he was an Indian, but not an abject servile Indian, rather a cultivated man, enhanced by work and who was aware of his strength and worth'). His behaviour is not in the least 'wild', and he doesn't remember his native language. At one point we are allowed a glimpse of the Aztec past, when the bandits hide out in an estate called Xochimancas, which had been a flower garden in pre-Columbian times.[14] But in the action of the novel, and for Nicolás, this heritage is as dead as 'Palenque or Pompeii', to use Altamirano's own examples. In its earliest stages, then, the Indian 'problem', which became a main preoccupation of Latin American novelists, was solved by drastic means. For the Brazilian Americanists could not help exposing their literary sympathy with Indians as merely extravagant, and the Aztec Altamirano barely left them with a physiognomy to be identified by.

Juan León Mera's *Cumandá* (1879), a 'drama among savages', announced a new start. The novel is made up of two largely independent stories. One concerns José Domingo de Orozco, a white landowner whose cruelty provokes an Indian rising led by a certain Tibón. After this rising, in which most of his family perishes, Orozco becomes a priest, and finally re-encounters Tibón back with his tribe in the depths of the forest, moribund but defiant: 'Ah white man, I know you, you are one of the tyrants of my race, you tortured and killed my parents. . .Since I can't rise to tear you apart, remove yourself'. Orozco's earnest entreaties, however, finally elicit a supreme tear from Tibón and presumed repentance. The other story is about the love felt by Orozco's son Carlos for Cumandá, who looks like the Indians she grew up with, but turns out to be Carlos's sister who had been snatched from the ruins of the family house by Tibón's band. The echoes of Bernardin de Saint Pierre's *Paul et Virginie*, and of Chateaubriand,[15] are persistent in this novel. The love-lorn Carlos wanders through America's wilds like another René, enchanted by the songs and beauty of Cumandá; for him, as for Paul and René, an unmovable barrier stands between him and the innocent woman he loves. Natural happiness is shown to be impossible for anyone who belongs to the civilized world. Mera differs from Bernardin de Saint Pierre and Chateaubriand however in setting his novel at home in Ecuador and in giving it an immediate geographical and historical context. In the story of father Orozco, which acts as a frame for Carlos's romance, we are furnished with such data as the exact altitude of Orozco's estate above sea level and the calendar dates of the Indian rising (which did happen), and are left in no doubt about the immediate significance of the events described. Explicit in Orozco's tactical and then moral victory over Tibón's people are both a tragedy and a national policy.

This same conflict appears in the novels of the Peruvian Clorinda Matto de Turner, though with less intervening romance. Her censure of the church, for supporting the oppressors of the Incas' descendants in the Andes, got her excommunicated, but her loyalty in the last instance was also to Christianity. She enters into her own novel *Birds without a Nest* (*Aves sin nido*, 1889), a 'tale of priestly corruption in Peru', barely disguised as the charitable Lucia, who like the repentant Orozco would save what she could of the Indian soul. (To this end, Matto de Turner later translated parts of the New Testament into Quechua.) Yet her sense of the tremendous degradation undergone by these survivors of the noble Inca civilization becomes so great that she is driven actually to desire their extinction:

> May it please God that one day, exercising His goodness,
> He may decree the extinction of the indigenous race, which
> after displaying imperial grandeur, swallows the filth of
> opprobrium. May it please God to extinguish them, for they
> cannot possibly recover their dignity or exercise their rights!

Matto de Turner was unquestionably a naive writer. But her exposure of such violent inner ambiguities greatly illuminates the contradictions inherent in much early Indianist writing. These reappear in Alcides Arguedas's *Race of Bronze* (*Raza de bronce*, 1919) in especially interesting fashion since Arguedas can be seen emending his attitudes and style as an Indianist writer in successive versions of the novel.[16] Arguedas was first attracted to the Indian as a magic figure, an avatar of the 'bronze race' of the Incas who carried within him the strangeness and exoticism of another ancient civilization. These were qualities made much of by the Modernists who influenced the young Arguedas, notably José Santos Chocano and Rubén Darío when they were not feeling despondent about the 'disastrous' legacy of Latin America's half-breed origins. But try as he would, Arguedas could not blot out the far more immediate spectacle of a hopeless and degraded Indian peasantry and proletariat whom, in the successive versions of his novel, he came to find more and more 'abominable'. Consistently with this, the one white character in the novel sympathetic to the Indians, Suárez, an author with Modernist leanings who resembles the younger Arguedas, is made to appear increasingly ridiculous and futile. By the end, Arguedas's pessimism is as negative as Matto de Turner's.

In the interwar years a way out of this impasse was provided by the spread of socialist ideas in Latin America. The theorists of the Mexican Revolution, and Marxist thinkers in the Andean republics in the 1920s (notably the Peruvian José Carlos Mariátegui), attributed a new role to the Indian in the history and destiny of Latin America. From being religious and racial, the Indian 'problem' became social and political. This new approach was reflected in numerous novels of the period, among them *El indio* (1935) by the Mexican Gregorio López y Fuentes, *Huasipungo* (1934) by the Ecuadorian Jorge Icaza and *Broad and Alien is the World* (*El mundo es ancho y ajeno*, 1941) by the Peruvian Ciro Alegría. But just as important as this political shift, and more fertile for the novel, was the general growth of knowledge about Indian cultures and, particularly, the re-discovery and appreciation of Indian literary texts. The fundamental difference between all the Indianist novels we have mentioned and the work of Miguel Ángel Asturias, José María Arguedas (no relation of Alcides) and Augusto Roa Bastos, to name three outstanding modern advocates of America's first inhabitants, is the degree to which Indian languages and literatures serve as a source of inspiration. Only quite recently have the classic texts of American Indian literature become readily available in translation into western languages. Americanist scholarship, begun in earnest in the late nineteenth

century, with time provided Latin American authors with an
intelligible guide to the cultures which had preceded theirs and
had survived, mysterious and inscrutable, to the present day.
There was now at least a chance of understanding the Indian in
his own ancestral terms, of discovering a firm basis lacking
hitherto, with the publication of texts like the Quechua *God and
Men of Huarochiri*, the Aztec *Legend of the Suns*, and the monumental narratives of the various Maya groups: the *Books of
Chilam Balam* from Yucatan, and from Guatemala the *Annals* of
the Cakchiquels and the *Popol vuh* of the Quiché, often called the
Bible of America. The nature of the influence exerted by these
and other texts has varied considerably from author to author, as
I show in later chapters. Here it is enough simply to record
the decisive effect of this rediscovered literature on the Latin
American novel.

5

To pretend that Latin American novelists, obsessed as some of
them may appear with exploring their own subcontinent, have
ever written in complete literary isolation would obviously be
preposterous. A list of literary models, in and outside Spanish
and Portuguese and beginning with Balzac, Sterne, Chateaubriand
and Dickens, would in modern times include Joyce, Faulkner,
Hamsun, Sartre and Robbe-Grillet. An especially important influence on modern novelists has been Jorge Luis Borges, a Latin
American author whose own literary erudition is encyclopaedic
(he was a professional librarian). His *Fictions* (*Ficciones*, 1944),
an oasis in the intellectual deserts of the Second World War, have
become a touchstone in western literature as a whole.

The novel has not been Borges's form, for reasons that are themselves of considerable interest. But his treatment of such basic
concepts as character, persona, plot, and setting, as in the celebrated 'fiction' 'Death and the Compass' for example, has profound implications for that form. Though he rarely mentions even
his most illustrious contemporaries, Carpentier or Asturias for
instance, it is clear that his fictions can have the effect of under-
mining the premise on which much of their work is based. The
part played by his fictions has been to question the novel as a

realist form, and to vindicate the larger possibilities of the prose narrative, possibilities often overlooked in the very origin of the novel, Cervantes's *Don Quixote*, as Borges has intimated in his own 'Cervantine' pieces ('Partial magic in *Don Quixote*', 'Pierre Menard, author of the *Quixote*', and others).

In particular, Borges's great intelligence and universalist stance have made it harder to maintain a simple-minded literary interest in exploring or exploiting what is 'indigenous' to Latin America. As a young admirer of Güiraldes, Borges once devoted himself to the gaucho, only later to divest and purge this figure of all geographical peculiarity. One of his fictions, 'The End', ostensibly serves as a coda to the poem *Martin Fierro* (1872–9), written by José Hernández to defend the gaucho against Sarmiento's presidential policies. But through repeated *tours de force* Borges makes it possible for us to read his story in complete ignorance of the original poem and lose nothing of importance thereby. He is *the* Latin American writer not in need of a local glossary. Again, in the vision seen in 'The Handwriting of God' by a priest, prostrate like so many of Borges's personae (including the witness of Martin Fierro's 'end'), he alludes to the Maya story of creation told in the *Popol vuh*. But this 'alien' text is allowed none of the special reverberations it has in Asturias's prose. Rather, along with Dante's *Divina Commedia*, it is so integrated into the structure of his fiction that problems of cultural relativism do not even notionally arise. Borges has described his position as an author in the following way:

> I believe that our tradition is the whole of western culture and I believe too that we have a greater right to that tradition than the inhabitants of other western nations. Argentinians, South Americans in general, can handle any European theme, handle it without superstition, with an irreverence which can have, and already has, fortunate consequences.[17]

This 'irreverence' is quintessentially that of the city: in Sarmiento's terms, Borges would be more European than the Europeans. What the city 'contains' for him belongs to a universal tradition going back to Babylon itself, that primary centre of commerce and translation, astronomy and literature which inspired such fictions as

'The library of Babel' and 'The lottery in Babylon'. If the disembodied intellectualism of the *Fictions* is 'beset' or 'proscribed' like Sarmiento's city, then it is lyrically and poignantly by man's absurd mortality alone, and not by geography and history, the traditional concerns of the realist novel.

Borges's importance for Latin American authors may be judged from the range of reactions he has provoked. These have sometimes been pointedly hostile. The nationalists and the Marxists of his own country, among them 'parricide' writers (to use Emir Rodríguez Monegal's word[18]) like David Viñas and Adolfo Prieto, have accused him of being irresponsibly cosmopolitan. And the Mexican Juan Rulfo is reported to have referred to him as 'that Englishman'. At the same time, his prose has proved the most fertile of precedents. The magnificent novella *Birthday* (*Cumpleaños*, 1969) by Carlos Fuentes, with its skilful transitions from character to type, its shifting perspectives in time and space, its conjunction of logic and geometry with passion ('algebra with fire'), undeniably owes much to the *Fictions*. Other modern writers of Latin America have engaged with Borges at the deepest level; indeed, some of the greatest of the new novels have benefited from his influence. Cortázar's *Hopscotch* (*Rayuela*) (and hence *Manuel's Book*) evolved in part from early short stories by that author which are most Borgesian in nature; and the character Aureliano Babilonia, who dominates the climactic closing chapters of García Márquez's *One Hundred Years of Solitude*, bears many of the traits which distinguish the personae of the *Fictions*.

At this point in the story of Latin American prose, the fundamental works of Sarmiento and da Cunha, my starting place, no doubt seem remote. And their initial formulations have indeed been continuously modified by the historical and literary developments alluded to above. Yet the echo of Sarmiento's phrase: 'which I will call South American', used to designate his antagonist and antithesis, was slow to die. In fact, only in the modern novels of Latin America has the relationship of the author to his continental environment undergone radical transformation.

MIGUEL ÁNGEL ASTURIAS

'Gaspar Ilóm lets them rob the land of Ilóm of the sleep of its eyes.

Gaspar Ilóm lets them tear out with an axe the eyelids of the land of Ilóm. . .

Gaspar Ilóm lets them scorch the branches of the eyelashes of the land of Ilóm with the fires that turn the moon the colour of an old ant. . .'

Gaspar Ilóm moved his head from one side to the other. To deny, crush the accusation of the earth he was sleeping on with his *petate* [mat], his shadow, his wife, buried with his dead and his umbilical cord, unable to escape a snake with six hundred thousand coils of mud, moon, woods, rain, mountains, lakes, birds and thunder which he felt around his body.

'The land falls dreaming from the stars, but awakes where the mountains were, today Ilóm's bald ridges, where the *guardia* sings with ravine sobs, the hawk flies on its head, the termite walks, the dove moans, and he sleeps with his *petate*, his shadow and his wife, the one who should slash the eyelids of those who chop down the trees, should burn the eyelashes of those who scorch the land and should chill the bodies of those who catch the water of the rivers which dreams as it flows and sees nothing but which caught in pools opens its eyes and sees all with a deep gaze. . .'

Gaspar stirred, sat up and began again to move his head from one side to the other to crush the accusation of the earth, bound to sleep and death by the snake of six hundred thousand coils of mud, moon, woods, rain, mountains, lakes, birds and thunder which was squeezing his bones and turning him into a mass of black kidney beans; a night of depths was raining down.

And he heard, with the holes of his ears he heard:

'Yellow rabbits in the sky, yellow rabbits in the forest, yellow rabbits in the water will fight beside Gaspar. The war of Gaspar Ilóm will begin, he being carried along by his blood, by his river, by his speech of blind knots. . .'

The word of the ground, made into solar flame, was about to burn the gopher ears of the yellow rabbits in the sky, the yellow rabbits in the woods, the yellow rabbits in the water; but Gaspar was becoming earth falling from where earth falls, that is, dream-sleep that finds no shadow to dream on the ground of Ilóm and the solar flame was impotent, with its voice mocked by the yellow rabbits who suckled themselves on a pawpaw tree, changed into pawpaws, which clung to the sky, changed into stars, and spread out in the water like reflections with ears.

Naked earth, wakened earth, maize earth in need of sleep, Gaspar who was falling from where the earth falls, maize earth bathed by rivers of water stinking from being awake so long, of green water in the sleeplessness of the forests sacrificed for maize made man the sower of maize. From the start the maiceros went ahead with their burning and their axes in forests of ancestral shade, two hundred thousand young ceiba trees a thousand years old.

Hombres de maíz (Buenos Aires, 1949). *Men of Maize.*
Opening paragraphs.

From the very first moments of Asturias's novel, the reader is immersed in a recognizably 'different' world. We do not know who speaks the three opening sentences, incantatory and sonorous (more so in Spanish). We gather that the land of Ilóm is being spoilt because of the inactivity of Ilóm himself. The details of this desecration, of eyes, eyelids, eyelashes, make it (the land) seem more alive than its owner. Then, when we see Ilóm lying there, saying 'no' with his head, we realize that the accusation is being uttered by the land itself, the first speaker in the novel.

Ilóm denies the charge but cannot avoid hearing it, in a mental state that is as much dream as waking: even when he sits up later he merely 'stirs' and goes on moving his head without necessarily awakening out of sleep into a more 'real' world. Lying or sitting up, he is bound to the earth as to a mother, by the innumerable serpentine coils which constrict movement and escape. These coils are formed of the strange but real phenomena of his natural surroundings. When the earth speaks a second time, the 'they' of the opening become more specific: the despoilers who as they scorch and chop down vegetation (eyelashes) and dam up flowing water (weeping eyes covered by eyelids) force an awareness of the atrocities they commit. The third incantatory speech promises him, if he resists, help of cosmic proportions, so that he himself will be reimmersed and borne along in the flow of existence, and no longer be the static, bound and passive creature we first encounter. His cyclic reality, from being constrictive, becomes rapid and initiatory, with the metamorphic example of the rabbits who, yellow like 'maize made man', resist, mock and prevail like guerrillas darting unpredictably in and out of natural cover.

This progression of events, as such, superbly matches the narrative pace. From the verbs applied to Ilóm himself, we learn in measured stages that he nods, stirs and hears; and the three appeals of the earth, from a repetitive 'timeless' start, grow urgent in the final close conjunction of 'will fight', 'will begin'. Further, though the earth's speeches to Ilóm are formally distinguished by quotation marks from the narrator's intervening words about him, there is a great rhythmic and lexical similarity between the two sets of three paragraphs, each with their internal triadic patterns. Speech and action form a 'stream of consciousness' as in Virginia Woolf, or James Joyce (whom Asturias has translated), with no 'exterior' term of comparison: we cannot not be involved in the transactions between 'Ilóm' and 'the land of Ilóm'. Most aptly, this similarity diminishes as Ilóm begins to react and respond as a creature in his own right. For, as the passage proceeds, Ilóm becomes more active. A pull of alcohol and a brief and violent coupling with his wife foster this sensation of selfhood, and of existence within his 'species and tribe'. Finally, in his own words, he announces his decision to assert himself and resist.

Up to this point we have been given very little information about who Ilóm is or who his enemies are. But his curiously deformed Spanish, our glimpse of his 'hungry idol's face', the numerous native Indian words (explained in a glossary) which run through his thoughts, and the fact that for him land and water

are live forces and, as the very title of the novel has already indicated, that men are made of maize, combine to present him as a
Maya Indian, a survivor of a major pre-Columbian culture and
economy, ever more vulnerable to the intrusion of foreigners. The
intruders here come more sharply into focus precisely when Ilóm
decides to shoot them down, an action reported with notable
laconism. They are the *maiceros* who burn large tracts of bush in
order to grow maize for profit, and not as part of the necessary and
sacred ritual by which maize men may nourish themselves: the
mixed-blood *ladinos*, whose loyalties are not to the Maya but to
the white descendants of the Spanish conquistadors, in Asturias's
native Guatemala and other parts of Middle America settled by the
Maya thousands of years ago. In other words, the characters of
Asturias's narrative merge only as the reasons for their antagonism
emerge, different ideas about agricultural practice and competition
for available land. These reasons in turn are not put forward for
themselves but are drawn out of profounder differences in religious
belief, historical experience and ways of perceiving the world.

At first Ilóm's war goes well and he is believed 'invincible' by
his people. For a moment they find relief and recover abundance
in their ancient and 'magic' part of the New World. And at the
feast which celebrates Ilóm's triumph we share the perception of
the maize-men participants, witnessing an effective confluence of
human and vegetable flesh (alluded to also in the description of
the inactive Ilóm as a 'mass of black beans'). We thus understand
Ilóm's motives better, and the title of the novel itself. However,
this regained paradise doesn't last long: this feast is also Ilóm's
last supper. Through poison passed from the white colonel Godoy
(sent to quell the uprising), to Vaca Manuela, and from her to
her husband Tomás, an Indian 'untado de ladino' ('ladino-
tainted'), the Maya band is reduced and brutally dispersed. Gaspar
Ilóm is last seen throwing himself into the 'river' which mytho-
logically he himself becomes by his action.

The story of Gaspar Ilóm is the first of the six episodic sections
which make up *Men of Maize*. Its importance has been widely
recognized in criticism, for itself, in relation to the rest of the
novel, in the tradition of Indianist writing, and indeed in the history of the Latin American novel as a whole. Here a modern Latin
American writer can be seen approaching the dark unknown areas

of his culture, with a language capable of registering his discoveries. In his prose, Ilóm, as an 'Indian', is not a psychological or political postulate, a 'necessary' innocent. He speaks for himself, and shoots the *ladinos* because they profane a belief, expressed in the sacred writings of his forefathers, which in the last instance has to be accepted or rejected as true: 'Crops to eat are the sacred food of man who was made from maize. Crops for profit are the hunger of man who was made from maize', as the elders of Ilóm's community put it.

What then enabled Asturias to interpret the voice of his land with such precision? Part of the answer must lie in his familiarity at one and the same time with the folklore of Maya Indians, of the Quiché, Cakchiquel, Mam and other Maya language groups, who form the majority of Guatemala's population ('Quiché' in the Quiché language means the same as 'Guatemala', which derives from a Toltec-Nahuatl word for 'wood area'), and with the classic literary texts of the civilization from which that folklore derived. His first sustained contact with the Maya occurred during his early childhood, in the first years of this century, when his family, bourgeois and liberal in tendency, moved from the capital because of harassment by the notorious dictator Estrada Cabrera. In the courtyard of his family's country house he first heard, in broken Spanish, fragments of the ancestral myths and legends of the Maya. He was also able to observe at first hand the social and domestic customs of these people, as the practical effects of their beliefs. A detail like Ilóm's buried umbilical cord could be traced to this source, as could his attitude to his land and crops. The acutely physical sense of the despoliation of the land which its accusation of Ilóm conveys (the torn-out eyelids, the scorched eyelashes) is corroborated by studies of modern Maya folklore, and corresponds in detail with prayers like this one, collected by J. E. S. Thompson, and recited by people who still hesitate to spoil the land's 'face':

> O God my mother, my father, Lord of the Hills and
> Valleys, Spirit of the Forests, be patient with
> me for what I am about to do as I've always done. . .
> I'm going to dirty you [spoil your beauty]. I'm
> going to work you that I may live.[1]

And the fact that the earth may complain and solicit revenge for wrong usage is reminiscent of the warnings issuing from the maize stalks themselves, still heard by the Mam in this century, who as a result have refused to abandon their traditional *milpas* (maize fields) for paid work on plantations.

After Asturias had become a university student, and had been in contact with the Mexican José Vasconcelos[2] and other Latin Americans professing a sociological concern with the Indian 'race', these early experiences of his formed the substance of the thesis he presented on his investiture as a lawyer: *The Social Problem of the Indian (El problema social del indio)*, published in Guatemala City in 1923. Though the sympathies and the perspectives of his thesis differ extremely from those of *Men of Maize* (a point of some consequence which we take up later on), we can hardly fail to note the many marked similiarities between the problematic Indian of his early theorizing and Gaspar Ilóm. The manner in which Ilóm is bound by his beliefs–superstitions as a primitive agriculturist; the amazing stimulation that a pull of alcohol gives him; the rough way he makes love to his wife; the impassive, almost ceremonial deliberation with which he picks off the *ladinos*, as if they were so many sacrificial victims: all these traits are meticulously described as characteristic of Indians in Asturias's thesis, though as evidence for a different overall argument. The point is simply that already as a young man and nascent author, Asturias believed he knew the natives of his country well, and was prepared to expound their character, habits, speech, superstitions and so on. Had he attempted an Indianist *novel* at this stage, however, he would no doubt have written a Meso-American equivalent of Alcides Arguedas's *Race of Bronze*, and would have foundered on the dilemma made explicit in that book. Instead he went to Europe and learned a good deal more about the first heritage of America.

At the Sorbonne in the late 1920s Asturias became the student of Georges Raynaud, who was then working on a French translation of Maya texts from Guatemala. These included the monumental Quiché work, the *Popol vuh* or *Book of Counsel*, often referred to as the 'Bible of America' since the history of the Quiché there begins with a long genesis sequence, in which is related the creation of man from maize; and the *Annals* of their near neighbours the Cakchiquel. Written in their respective Maya languages, though in the Roman alphabet, during the Spanish colonial period, these texts were then being effectively discovered for the first time by the modern world, in translations like Raynaud's, a fortune shared at this time by several such texts of classic American Indian literature from other parts of the continent. In this situation Asturias had the double advantage of having lived close to the descendants of the Maya and of being one of very few Latin American authors to have any scholarly knowledge of classic native literature. And he didn't waste it. As well as producing Spanish versions of both the Quiché and the Cakchiquel text, from Raynaud's French, he published some *Legends of Guatemala* (*Leyendas de Guatemala*, 1930) of his own that were heavily influenced by Maya literature (that is, the two Guatemalan texts translated by him, and the Yucatecan *Book of Chilam Balam of Chumayel*, translated into Spanish by the Mexican Médiz Bolio).[3] These *Legends* marked the beginning of a specifically literary involvement with the Maya, which has endured throughout Asturias's long career as a writer.

As the primary episode in *Men of Maize*, on any account a major novel, the Gaspar Ilóm story undoubtedly benefited from this new literary knowledge of the Maya. Indeed, it would arguably have been impossible without it. Fused with the folklore of Asturias's youth, we find structures and principles which give Ilóm's world not just a coherence of its own, but dignity as well, qualities which are decidedly absent in *The Social Problem of the Indian*. The most obvious sign of change is of course the novel's title. Among other documents, the *Popol vuh* relates the successive creations of the world, the inadequacy and destruction of the men of clay, and the men of wood, and then the beauty of the maize men, the first of whom, Balam Quitze and his companions, were the forefathers of the Maya Quiché tribe. White and yellow maize ears are taken from Paxil, the place of abundance or sustenance, and are kneaded by the gods into human flesh, with the help of the goddess Ixcumane, until they are fat and strong. The perfection of these first actual men was such that their intelligence had to be dimmed to make them less than gods, and worshippers of gods, which they dutifully became, espousing beliefs the remnants of which prompt Ilóm's rebellion. The first translator of the *Popol vuh*, a Spanish priest called Ximénez found these tales 'childish'. In principle they are no more or less absurd than the Old Testament story of creation, believed literally by pre-Enlightenment Europe. This is part of the point Asturias is making in the Ilóm episode. In his thesis he had spoken of the need to 'combat the superstitions' of the Indian; now these 'superstitions' are granted the status of a cult or religion, equal to any other in the liberal order of things his own tolerance has always favoured.

Treating the Maya creation story as 'adult' literature enabled Asturias to find reason in a behaviour and a mentality he had previously considered degenerate and sadly incoherent. The exuberant sensuality of Ilóm's feast, for example, repugnant no doubt to one used to bourgeois table manners, depends chiefly on the excitement Asturias had been trained to hear in the harmony between human and vegetable flesh. His prose flourishes prodigiously with this newly-found mode of perception, as Ilóm and his people again enjoy the abundance of Paxil, the 'Place of Sustenance', as it is remembered, where maize and man came from. This perception extends to the language-play and allusiveness characteristic of the classic texts, which rely precisely on the identity of the human with the vegetable body. Observed by adolescents with 'gourd faces', the men at the feast ask the women to bring them *tamales* of green corn like the flesh of the 'unhardened maize lad'. There are puns on the words for boy (*munal*) and young maize (*mun nal*) in the *Book of Chilam Balam of Chumayel*, in which text the request for a *yucca* runs: 'Bring me a woman with a very white and well-rounded calf; here will I tuck back her skirt from her calf' (i.e. peel it). The reasons for Ilóm's hostility to the sacrilegious *maiceros* and *ladinos* are thus not just explained, but lived through in the narrative itself.

Again, if we consider the refrain that conveys Ilóm's constriction and passivity (the '600,000 coils. . .'), the run of nouns is odd, unfamiliar and disconnected enough to appear a jumble, even nonsense, in a less charged context. And the Indian of Asturias's thesis, in his 'sociopathic' state, is described as physically inert and barely articulate. In the Cakchiquel *Annals*, Asturias found a refrain, which no doubt served as a model for his own, as he skilfully causes it to interact with what he has given us so far, to produce not just the 'poetry' critics have remarked upon, a prose that appears poetic in an alien European language like Spanish or English, but concepts essential and necessary to Ilóm's world: 'mud, moon, woods, rain, mountains, lakes, birds and thunder'. The Cakchiquel refrain has a very similar function, and evokes both the fear *and* the capacity to inspire fear proper to the forefathers of the tribe as they set out for Guatemala as warriors from Tula: 'And there came wasps, bees, mud, darkness, rain, clouds, mist'. Further, when Ilóm succeeds in asserting himself as the 'Invincible', the hero of his kind and his tribe, his courage is oddly but powerfully described in words from the *Annals* which play on the root of the term *xahil*, dance, which is also the family after whom the *Annals* are named in Asturias's translation: 'great is his strength, great is his dance.' And the guerrilla rabbits, who incite Ilóm to rebel and promise help, are reinforced by their relations in the *Popol vuh* (lines 4060–90) who help the Twins Hunahpu and Ixbalanque in their struggle against the murderous Lords of the Underworld, Xibalba. An especially neat example of how reading Maya literature enhanced Asturias's view of the Maya he knew comes in the passage describing Ilóm's draught of alcohol, which literally 'separated his head from his body'. Alcoholism was one of the Indian vices most severely censured by the young Asturias. In *Men of Maize* he was able to relate this need and Ilóm's stimulation to those passages in the *Popol vuh* which (in Raynaud's translation at least) tell of Ixcumane's gift of spirit to the first maize men, and of the heroic father of the magic twins, Hun Hunahpu, who at one point can perceive better as a result of having his head severed from his body (lines 2203–2296).

Even when he had still thought of Guatemalan Indians as just a social problem, Asturias had taken care to note that, however abject they are today, the Maya of his country had valiantly resisted the Spanish conquistadors and had inflicted heavy losses on them. Reading Quiché and Cakchiquel literature showed him how the struggle felt from the other side, and how the atrocities committed by the invaders appeared to the Maya. By a narrative device used to great effect in the Ilóm story, he relates their present resistance to that of their ancestors. During the communal celebration of Ilóm's triumph, the 'old men' recall how El Avilantaro, the Indian name for Cortes's companion, the conquistador Pedro de Alvarado, had snatched gold and murdered chieftains, and describe him as the first propagator of the white or 'Latin' poison. This is the moment in the novel at which a historical consciousness is most developed. From the timeless incantations of the opening, we have moved to action (the shooting down of the *maiceros*), and to an understanding of that action in terms not just of tribal philosophy and religion, but as tribal history.

More important still, we can say that as a result of his Parisian education Austurias was able to create Ilóm, who is a character unprecedented in the Latin American novel.[4] Expressing assumptions no doubt shared by others less ready to admit them, Asturias had once written (in his early thesis): 'the indigenous peoples lack cohesion; in them as in their individuals, the subject is missing and the person doesn't exist'. And he had referred to the 'absurd' traditions of the Indians, which could perpetuate no more than 'shadows'. During his finest hour at least, Ilóm is anything but a shadow and very much a historical subject. All this is worth emphasizing because such achievements turn out to be extremely rare in Asturias's fiction, a fact which distinguishes the Ilóm episode as perhaps his most innovatory and successful piece of writing.

Asturias has often described himself as a 'committed' writer, who will not be a 'vestal' or an 'Ariel'[5] but involves himself in the problems of his time and place. As far as his Indian compatriots are concerned, classic Maya literature may be credited with having provoked in him the change of heart we have witnessed in Gaspar Ilóm's story. In his university thesis his solution of the Indian problem had been tantamount to genocide: a therapy which entailed European immigration on a scale grand enough to eradicate unwanted Indian genes, the internal policies of the U.S. and Argentina being proposed as exemplary in this respect. By creating for Ilóm the role he did, he suggests rather that Indian rebellion is not only justified but desirable, and that the Maya world is worthy of respect and capable of exerting the strongest fascination.

Defining his involvement, and with more than a hint of populism, Asturias has further spoken of his ambition to be the spokesman or great interpreter (*gran lengua*) of 'his tribe', the one who speaks generally for the oppressed of his country. His first published novel, *The President* (*El señor presidente*, 1946), unmistakably sprang from this source: the treatment which he, his family and Guatemala as a whole received at the hands of the notorious dictator Estrada Cabrera. Sympathy with the oppressed was also behind the so-called Banana Trilogy of novels of the 1950s: *Strong Wind* (*Viento fuerte*, 1950), *The Green Pope* (*El papa verde*, 1954), *The Eyes of the Buried* (*Los ojos de los enterrados*, 1960), which deals with the conflicts between native workers and the foreign capitalists introduced into the country by Estrada Cabrera. With Asturias's ingenious device of making the principal U.S. landowner in the novels a wholly good-natured if misguided befriender of the workers, the trilogy stands as a solid indictment, specifically of the United Fruit Company, which has also been the target of Neruda's invective. Criticism yielded to rage in the topical exposure *Weekend in Guatemala* (*Week-end en Guatemala*, 1956), a condemnation of the foreign-aided overthrow of Arbenz's government in 1954, which Asturias had tried hard to save in his capacity as a diplomat.[6]

This more overtly political writing returns us once more to the special place that the Ilóm story occupies in his work. For if we survey Asturias's other 'Indianist' works we find not just the absence of that commitment, but what appears to be a positive denial of it. In this sense the Maya pieces in his early *Legends of Guatemala*, notably the ballet 'Cuculcán', stand at the antipodes of his university thesis. They constitute, as Paul Valéry aptly put it,[7] a 'rêve tropique', with no effective connection with the waking world of social and political realities. The brilliant colour sequences and configurations of archetypes like the feathered serpent Cuculcán have more in common with the experimental art forms of Kandinsky and others in the 1920s than they have with historical Guatemala. How true this is may be judged by comparing 'Cuculcán' with the opening of *Men of Maize*, formally so similar (with their alternating paragraphs; patterns of 3×3, etc.): the 'legend' does not transcend exquisite movement on a small stage. By turns, Asturias is nostalgic and eclectic, taking what suits him from the most various sources, as he has done again in the poetic prose of *Three of the Four Suns* (1971, which quotes from the pre-Columbian codices of cultures quite alien to the Maya) and in his

long poem *Spring Vigil* (*Clarivigilia primeraveral*, 1965). Of course
any writer is free to be influenced as he pleases, by Maya or any
other literature. The point here is how differently he has used
and interpreted the same originals. The attempt to re-historicize
the *Popol vuh* in *Men of Maize* is altogether lacking in the mythic
Indian sequences we find inset into the Banana Trilogy, and goes
in exactly the opposite direction to what happens in a 'legend'
like 'Cuculcán'. For this feathered-serpent-figure has great historical significance, particularly in Yucatan, where after the collapse
of classic Maya civilization he was resisted as a leader of a Toltec
or Mexican invasion inimical to older Maya values. This is information of a kind which Asturias frequently not just ignores but
actively suppresses, here and in his more recent novels, *The
Mulatta and Mr Fly* (*Mulata de tal*, 1963), and *Maladrón* (1969)
ostensibly an 'epic of the Green Andes'. To this degree he invents
the folklore of the Maya on their behalf and alerts us to a
tendency in all his 'Indianist' writing.

At least, this view of Asturias seems to offer us most chance of
understanding what happens to Ilóm in the novel *Men of Maize*
taken as a whole. Ilóm certainly does not, and after his basic act of
rebellion, cannot survive as the protagonist. Once he has jumped
into the river he remains literally submerged. The remarkable
waking-dream we had entered in his company now, without him,
becomes definitively a dream, of happenings that are extravagant,
and in which the Indian world impinges in quite another way on
that of the *ladinos* and Colonel Godoy. Ilóm had after all shot the
maiceros. The fate of Godoy and others involved in the incident
is by contrast merely fantastic.

Formally, the rest of the novel consists of three episodes of
vengeance for Ilóm; an episode which delves deeper into the experiences of the woman María Tecun, whose family had been
involved in the original 'plot'; a final recapitulatory episode (the
lengthiest), and a brief epilogue. Each of the vengeances is followed through in detail that is not so much relentless as pictur-
esque. One character, Machajón, is bodily removed from earth on
his way to his lover, and becomes a star. The Zacatón family, the
pharmacists who supplied the poison, become a row of grinning
skulls. Colonel Godoy is magically incinerated. Now all these
deaths occur in mysterious ways: we no longer have a clear sense

of conflict between the Indians' world and that of their oppressors, between their respective 'camps', as it were. No doubt this is part of Asturias's point: that with the decline of Indian culture all becomes confused and loses the cohesion which Ilóm was momentarily able to give his people. However, Asturias seems to want it both ways, for in the same breath this avenging of Ilóm is announced as a programme sanctioned by the Maya gods themselves, no less:

> Light of the sons, light of the tribes, light of
> the race, before your face let it be said
> that the carriers of white-rooted poison should have
> the *pixcoy* [a bird of ill omen] to the left of their roads.

The *ladinos* are thus subject to an omnipotence reported in the *Popol vuh* (lines 75–85) to be that of the 'Former, the Shaper, light of the tribes, light of the sons, light of the race'. But as the author of that classic text freely conceded, Maya religion had long ago ceased to be an all-powerful social and political force. The use, then, of Maya literature here is of quite a different order from that of the particular local examples we noted in the Ilóm episode itself. For to be effective the grand-sounding curse relies not on the action of characters who are shown both to remember their past and to exist in the modern world, but on unseen witchcraft and magic. The agencies of the magic are accordingly shadow or dream figures, when they are figures at all, whose validity is guaranteed and tested only in Asturias's imagination.

Much has been made, and rightly, of the magic realism of Asturias's writing, and his sense of what Carpentier called 'lo real maravilloso americano' or the marvellous reality of America. And in the later episodes of *Men of Maize*, as in more recent novels like *The Mulatta and Mr Fly* and *Maladrón*, he is unquestionably adept at intermingling Indian perceptions of the world with the luxuriant varieties of colonial baroque which so fascinate him. He is by turns solemn, brusquely humorous and extravagant, in a prose that offers a surfeit of sensation. But the term 'magic realism' ceases to be useful as soon as it doesn't help us to distinguish between those moments in his writing where, as with Ilóm, an effort is made to integrate myth with history, and those where myth is a repast for itself. This above all else is the distinction which militates against the overall consistency of *Men of Maize*, the 'unity' of the novel as a whole having been the subject of much debate.[8]

By the sixth and last episode of *Men of Maize*, 'Coyote Mail' Asturias writes as if himself conscious of the problem of artistic unity and he palpably endeavours to give things an overall coherence once again. Here the mail carrier, Nicho Aquino, descends to the underworld to be confronted with his *nagual*, his animal double; this confrontation, undeniably essential to Middle-American myth from ancient to modern times, is then turned into a device for opposing western and Maya truth. Nicho is said to shed his old self, and then is put through a series of 'tests', much as Hunahpu and Ixbalanque were by the Lords of Xibalba in the *Popol vuh* (lines 3431–900). By now, however, Asturias is not hesitating to create his own Maya folklore. With the eclecticism we mentioned earlier, he intercalates, in his own way, these underworld tests with the successive creations of man narrated elsewhere in the *Popol vuh* (lines 325–666; 4709–22). So that when Nicho and his companion emerge, appropriately on the fourth day, it is with the revelation 'that they are not clay men, that the sad puppets of sloppy mud were destroyed...that they are not wood men, that they are not puppets of the woods'. Asturias then allows them back up to the 'real world':

> where maize awaits them in every form, in the flesh of their children, who are of maize; in the bones of their dead who are of dried maize-husk; in the flesh of their women, maize moistened for contentment, because maize in the flesh of a young woman is like the seed dampened by the earth, when it is about to sprout; in the sustenance which there and then, after they wash in communal baths, they take to replenish their strength...

This elaborate and belated attempt on Asturias's part to point up the meaning of the novel is followed by a summary and explanation of its general plot. There could be no clearer measure of the distance we have strayed from the first brief living-out of Ilóm's economy.

Asturias began *Men of Maize* by relating the Maya literature he had encountered as a scholar to an existing social and political situation. This alone earns him an important place in Latin American literary history, and announces possibilities exploited, among others, by the Nicaraguan poet Ernesto Cardenal in his *Homage to the American Indians* (*Homenaje a los indios americanos*, 1969) and, more purposefully, by those Guatemalan guerrillas whose propaganda equates the Lords of Xibalba with U.S. imperialists.[9] But as a novelist and 'interpreter of his tribe' he did not carry further the achievement of the Gaspar Ilóm story, an exceptional gesture in his work. Augusto Roa Bastos, a native of the bi-lingual state of Paraguay (Guarani and Spanish), and José María Arguedas of Peru are, for example, authors who have shown more concern than he to express the predicament of Indians now, with their live oral and written traditions, and with the transformation and new birth of sustaining Indian myths. They undeniably share with Asturias admiration for 'classical' Indian literature: in this respect ancient Guarani liturgy and pre-Columbian Quechua are for Roa Bastos and Arguedas what the old Maya books are for the Guatemalan. However, both the later writers have been more preoccupied with showing what, if anything, such texts do and can mean in the world now.

These writers persistently follow ancient literature through into the shapes Indians themselves continue to give it, so that their writings are distinguished by the presence of living songs and phrases, in their original language, which both inform the Indians' lives and impregnate the Spanish narrative at the deepest level. These two authors have not just opposed the truths of conflicting myths and economies, western and Indian, but have striven to interpret the continuing results of that conflict, for example, in the messianism deriving from the Guarani Cult of the Dead in the case of Roa Bastos;[10] and with Arguedas, in a passionate corpus of songs and legends, including that post-Hispanic creation, the headless 'Inkarrey', awaiting the moment to reorganize and recover traditional Quechua values. There is eloquence enough in the fact that Roa Bastos would not claim to have achieved a full novel form, as an Indianist writer:[11] *Son of Man* (*Hijo de hombre*, 1959) remains painfully inconclusive and discrete. More significantly, Arguedas was driven to suicide largely because he could not sustain the vision of survival announced in *The Deep Rivers* (*Los ríos profundos*) and *Every Blood* (*Todas las sangres*). As for

Asturias, he did not allow himself to become entangled in the 'blind knots' of Ilóm's speech. This reluctance may be due as much to the linguistic and social fragmentation of the Guatemalan Maya (greater than that of the Quechua or the Guarani) as to Asturias's own confessed failure ever to learn a Maya language.

Innovatory and uneven as it is, *Men of Maize* has generally been found a difficult novel to read and assess. An earlier novel of Asturias's, *The President*, has proved less disconcerting no doubt because attempting less it succeeds more confidently. It provides a further insight into Asturias's creative strengths as a novelist. For, although few traces now remain, *The President*, too, began as an excursion into American Indian literature. Another sequence in the *Popol vuh* shaped his presentation of Estrada Cabrera's dictatorship in early drafts of the work. The dictator was identified with Tohil, a sinister god who demanded human blood in return for the gift of fire, youthful strength and position: by serving him, hunting and waylaying victims, the ancestors of the Quiché's leaders (of Toltec-Mexican provenance) for a time instituted a reign of terror among their fellows. Already we see that the connection with Indian myth is much more straightforward than in *Men of Maize*. Tohil–Estrada Cabrera is detestable, a creature of superstition and unholy order. The problem of venturing into an unknown world as an apologist simply doesn't arise. Moreover from being the inspiration of the whole story, Tohil had his role steadily reduced in rewritings between 1925 and 1946. At first his name was the title of the novel. But he ended up by dominating no more than an 'inexplicable' vision seen by the President's favourite, Angel Face, at the close of chapter thirty-seven. Correspondingly, Asturias came to account for the dictator's mythical power and its traumatic effects in terms and language which did not involve the exploration of 'alien' cultures. While in many respects similar to the opening of *Men of Maize*, in their presentation of a bemusing 'total' atmosphere, the first paragraphs of *The President* did not go beyond innovations made elsewhere in the western novel, by Joyce for example. I give the Spanish as well because of its strong phonetic qualities which defy translation:

. . .Alumbra, lumbre de alumbre, Luzbel de piedralumbre!
Como zumbido de oidos persistía el rumor de las campanas

a la oración, maldoblestar de la luz en la sombra, de la
sombra en la luz. Alumbra, lumbre de alumbre, Luzbel de
piedralumbra, sobre la podredumbre! Alumbra, lumbre de
alumbre, sobre la podredumbre, Luzbel de piedralumbre!
Alumbre alumbra, lmbre de alumbre. . ., alumbre. . .,
alumbra. . ., alumbra, lumbre de alumbre. . ., alumbra,
alumbre. . .

Los pordioseros se arrastraban por las cocinas del mercado,
perdidos en la sombra de la Catedral helada, de paso hacia
la Plaza de Armas, a lo largo de calles tan anchas como
mares, en la ciudad que se iba quedando atrás íngrima
y sola.

. . .Boom, bloom, alum-bright, Lucifer of alunite! The sound
of the church bells summoning people to prayer lingered on,
like a humming in the ears, an uneasy transition from
brightness to gloom, from gloom to brightness. Boom, bloom,
alum-bright, Lucifer of alunite, over the sombre tomb!
Bloom, alum-bright, over the tomb, Lucifer of alunite! Boom,
boom, alum-bright. . .bloom. . .alum-bright. . .bloom, alum-
bright. . .bloom, boom.

The beggars were shuffling past the market eating-houses
in the shadow of the frozen cathedral, on their way to the
Plaza de Armas, along streets as broad as seas, in the city
that was gradually left behind them, isolated and alone.[12]

The unease afflicting the President's country (never explicitly
named as Guatemala) emanates from the ominous noise and light
of this passage, and, in Joycean fashion, from the neologism
maldoblestar (where *malestar* means unease, *doble* double and
doblar to toll). Ears cannot hear anything beyond the booming of
the bells, while the light, ambiguous and uncertain, anticipates the
Luciferian character of Angel Face himself ('beautiful and evil as
Satan'). Bemused by these waves of sound and light, the beggars,
the 'rottenness below', feel a contradiction that goes still deeper,
as they drag themselves between the heat of the kitchens and the
ice of the house of the Señor (in Spanish, both God and the Lord
President). But the whole is viewed in the perspective of a nightmare; at one moment the streets are broad and unending as seas;

then, in giddy recession, the city is compressed into a lonely, isolated event.

Contradictions and distortions of this kind abound in the novel and are inexorably referred to their cause, the President at the centre who manipulates the lives of his subjects down to the last detail, in his sick hunger for power. He invades their last privacy, their 'most secret entrails'. The fear he and his agents inspire corrodes every civilized bond and robs the most intimate act of all dignity. Vasquez and La Masacuata, puppets of Angel Face, wither physically to 'a strand of garlic' as they roll coupled on the floor. As he emerges from Angel Face's house, fear reduces the proud bearing of General Canales to the scurrying trot of 'an Indian' (here an obviously demeaning comparison!) and makes a safe corner ahead recede abruptly into the distance. This spectacle of degrading oppression becomes yet more grotesque when the President, at last presented directly to the reader, turns out to be a trivial figure devoid of all presence, a shadow, someone there was no need to have been scared of anyway.

Asturias has spoken of the deep impression made on him by Estrada Cabrera at his trial: an inoffensive, sad man; people refused to believe he was the 'real' President. And the degree to which Asturias delights in 'exposing' this historical figure suggests how radical his scepticism towards myth can be, be it the myth of an all-powerful Tohil or the myth of man's creation out of maize. *The President* confirms the values dearest to Asturias, once a law student and son of a magistrate and school teacher. It is highly significant that the only positive touchstones in the nightmare of the novel coincide with the eminent rationality of his own political ideas. The 'revolutionary' programme which General Canales could not carry out because of the President's tyranny follows Asturias's own recipe for Guatemala item for item (reallocation of land, co-operatives for the import of agricultural machinery, popular control of the press, religious tolerance, popular education to eradicate superstition and foster civic virtue, and so on); and the student facing silence and madness in one of the President's gaols bravely goes on talking like an ideal product of the Popular University Asturias helped to found in the 1920s.[13] Further, the deepest profanation by the President is, by implication of the middle-class interior, the domestic heart of the bourgeoisie. It is hard to miss the sense of outrage, personal affront even, in the scene when Canales's daughter Camila is abducted by Angel Face's agents and the house is wrecked: 'And without further ado they checked the cupboards from top to bottom, breaking off the veneers, shooting up the mirrors and smashing the inlaid wood to splinters; others, lost in the large room, knocked over the chairs, the tables, the cabinets with photographs on them, tragic packs of cards in the darkness, or pounded on the grand piano which had been left open and which smarted like an ill-used animal each time they hit it.'

As the incarnation of myth and superstition, the President and his agents are blindly inimical to a real and sane order of things, here abused and tragically threatened. As novelistic 'material', myth remains 'outside', something detachable, defined by its otherness and its incompatibility. After being snatched from her true home, Camila is fascinated by Angel Face, and the spectacle of the President blessing their eventual union actually kills her worthy father, the General, outright. As she is removed she is shown literally passing out into another world, as the companion of one whose dubiousness and amorality are notorious, with his 'face of golden marble, fair hair, small mouth and a womanly air in violent contrast with the black of his manly eyes'. Asturias reports that in early versions the rape of Camila was to be a cause of indignation, further condemnation of an infernal leader. Later he learnt to postpone moral judgement and showed the alluring side of the President's 'insane' and superstitious world. The love of Camila and Angel Face acquires an excitement of its own, reminiscent of the surrealist pages of André Breton's *L'Amour fou*; and, more pointedly, of Gaspar Ilóm's trance-like perceptions (falling from sleep; separated head; maize as the body's core):

> Angel Face encircled her waist with his arm and led her along a path which fell from the warm sleep of the trees. They were aware of their heads and their throats; everything else, legs and hands, floated with them, among orchids and gleaming lizards, in the half-light, which slowly became dark talcum honey as they went further into the forest. Camila felt her body through her fine blouse like a soft milky moist seed through a tender maize leaf.

The sexual palpitation increases steadily, emanating always from the mysterious aura round Angel Face, and Camila goes further from herself into it, we are told 'from one life into another'.

Yet at a crucial moment this strange and magic nature becomes too much for her. A slug falls from her towel on to her skin and she shivers in revulsion: 'She didn't like it any more: the whole forest frightened her, its sweaty breath, its sleepless slumber, were slug-like'. In her recoil she remembers her old, normal self. This is like the sexton in *The Mulatta and Mr Fly* who shudders in the slime of snails crawling over him murmuring 'We want to be born, we want to be born': a white man exposed and suddenly scared in the teeming uninhibitedness of Indian reality; and again it is like the conquistador in *Maladrón* who is overwhelmed by his experience of untamed, magic Guatemala to the point of suffocation. That is, Canales's daughter is indelibly marked by her (and Asturias's) known world, and cannot escape for ever into the magic forest, believing her body to be tender American maize. In short, it is just because it exists beyond the pale that this strange world can serve as the habitat of both the President's agents and the disinherited Indians of Guatemala. But while in *The President* Asturias had opposed superstition and exposed myth (through characters like Canales, Camila and the student), he began *Men of Maize* by vindicating Ilóm, in an act of extraordinary moral and imaginative power.

ALEJO CARPENTIER

For several days the little squadron – comprising *La Décade* and *La Tintamarre*, in addition to the brig – sighted no other shipping, and seemed to be engaged on a pleasure cruise, rather than bound on a mission of aggression. They would drop anchor in a cove, furl the sails, and the sailors went ashore, some for firewood, others for clams – which were so numerous that they could be found three inches down in the sand – and took advantage of the occasion to lounge about amongst the *uvero* trees on the beach, or to bathe in a creek. The clarity, transparency, and coolness of the water, so early in the day, produced in Esteban an exaltation very like a state of lucid intoxication. Floundering about within his depth, he learned to swim, and could never bring himself to return to the shore when it was time to do so; he felt so happy, so enveloped and saturated by the light, that sometimes, back on dry land, he had the dazed, tottering gait of a drunken man. He called this his 'water-drunkenness', and afterwards offered his naked body to the ascending sun, lying on his stomach in the sand, or face upwards, arms and legs splayed as if crucified, with such an expression of joy on his face that he looked like some fortunate mystic, favoured with an ineffable vision.

On occasions, inspired by the fresh energy which this life was infusing in him, he undertook long explorations of the cliffs, clambering, jumping, paddling – marvelling at the things he discovered at the foot of the rocks. There were the pulpy leaves of the madrepore; the speckled, pitcher-shaped apples of the cowries; the slender cathedral architecture of certain shells, which, with their wings and needle-points, could only be seen in terms of the Gothic; the beaded whorls of the sea periwinkles, the Pythagorean convolutions of the

spindle-shell – the simulation with which many shells
concealed in their depths the splendour of a weld-painted
palace under the humble plaster of their exterior. At this
human step the sea-urchin proffered its black spines, the
timid oyster closed, the star-fish shrank, and the sponges,
attached to some submerged rock, swayed amidst rippling
reflections. In this prodigious Island Sea, even the pebbles
of the ocean bed had style and spirit; some were so perfectly
round that they looked as if they had been turned on a
lapidary's lathe; others were abstract in shape, but seemed
to dance with excitement, to be lifted, lengthened, turned
into arrows, by a sort of impulse springing from the matter
itself. There was translucent rock, with the clarity of
alabaster; rock like violet-coloured marble; granite, across
which the light danced under the water; and humble rocks,
bristling with sea-snails – whose seaweed-flavoured flesh the
young man extracted from their tiny green-black shells with
a cactus spine.

The most prodigious cacti mounted guard on the flanks
of these Hesperides without names where the ships put in
on their adventurous course: tall candelabra, panoplies with
green helms, green pheasants' tails, green swords, green
burrs, hostile water-melons, trailing quinces with spines
hidden beneath their deceptive smoothness. This was a
distrustful world, ready to inflict pain, but ever torn on
giving birth to some red or yellow flower, offered to man at
the cost of a prick, along with the treacherous gift of an Indian
fig or a prickly pear, whose flesh could be reached at last
if he tricked his way through a last palisade of eager spines.

In contrast to this vegetation armed with spikes, which
prevented access to certain of the hill-tops crowned with
ripe anonas, there was the Cambrian world down below:
infinite and multifarious forests of coral, with their textures
of flesh, lace and wool, their blazing auriferous, transmuted
trees: alchemical trees out of some book of spells or hermetic
treatise; nettles whose undersides one could not touch;
flamboyant ivy, twined in counterpoints and rhythms so
ambiguous that all delimitation between the inert and the
palpitant, the vegetal and the animal, was abolished. Amidst

a growing economy of zoological forms, the coral forests preserved the earliest baroque of Creation, its first luxuriance and extravagance, hiding their treasures where, in order to see them, man would have to imitate the fish he had once been, before he was shaped by the womb, yearning for the gills and tail which would have enabled him to choose these gorgeous landscapes as his permanent dwelling-place. In these coral forests Esteban saw a tangible image, a ready – and yet so inaccessible – configuration, of a Paradise Lost, where the trees, barely named as yet by the torpid, hesitant tongue of the Child-Man, would be endowed with the apparent immortality of these sumptuous flora, this ostensory, this burning bush, where autumn and spring could be detected only in a variation in the colours, or a slight shifting in the shadows.

El siglo de las luces (Havana 1962). Translated by John Sturrock as *Explosion in a Cathedral* (London 1963); translation here slightly modified. Chapter 3, section 24.

Of the three or four main characters in Alejo Carpentier's novel *Explosion in a Cathedral*, Esteban is the one chosen to guide us through a world especially dear to his author: the 'theological archipelago of the Caribbean', as it is called, the luminous heart of America to which both author and character, as Cubans, belong. In the brig *L'Ami du peuple* with her two attendant ships, Esteban escapes to the ocean on an American 'odyssey', from the port of Pointe à Pitre in Guadeloupe, where his former friend Victor Hugues, a champion of the French Revolution, is establishing his historical reputation as 'the Robespierre of the Isles'. As a child Esteban had grown up in a sheltered bourgeois mansion in Havana, cousin and friend of Carlos and Sofia. Like them, he was left unprotected on the death of their father, a rich merchant. At this point he fell under Hugues's influence and became his secretary. However, again like Carlos and Sofia, he did not remain entranced by him for long. Before setting sail Esteban is said to be sick of the cruelty and opportunism displayed by Hugues in his small but distinctive role in the vast concatenation of events prompted by the Revolution of 1789. At a primary level the novel may indeed be understood to be about those events: six long chapters divide a sequence of 47 sections which record revolutionary tumult and worse in a wide variety of settings in Europe (Paris, Bayonne) and America, and culminate in the rising against the French in Madrid on the 2nd of May 1808. Presented thus with some of the historical consequences of the 'Century of Enlightenment', we might be excused for detecting a certain sarcasm[1] in the original title of the novel, *El siglo de las luces*, which is the Spanish term for that period of European thought. From the start, however, we are made aware of a deeper meaning. It is not just the bloody practical effects of the Revolution which upset Esteban, but the wholesale transplanting of European ideologies to the New World. The relief he experiences on sailing away from the tricolors at Pointe à Pitre is also that of one entering another luminous world, to which he more properly belongs.

As the squadron sails out, beyond the sight of other shipping, the narrative pace slows down. In escaping the 'terrible scansion of the guillotine' (brought by Hugues to the Caribbean), Esteban and his few companions enter another rhythm of life. The verbs relax into the imperfect, even the future conditional tense (a change sometimes awkward to render in English). And in the newly-found solitude of the group, Esteban separates himself still further from the life which had caught him up. Alone, and quite naked, he literally immerses himself in his natural surroundings. The sensations registered by his body could hardly be more immediate. Thus 'enveloped and saturated' he is favoured with the perception of a 'fortunate mystic', the dominant quality of his vision being light. But in nature and origin this light differs altogether from the Enlightenment of Hugues. So that insofar as 'siglo' can also mean the secular, the terrestrial world, we see that the novel's title may refer just as much to this crucial experience of Esteban's, which occurs at the central moment in the narrative (section 24). At the point when he relinquishes himself to his own environment he may explore himself most fully, buoyed up and fulfilled as he never was as a student of Hugues's philosophy.

In proportion as we enter Esteban's vision and 'marvel' with him at his discoveries, he nevertheless becomes the most flexible and evanescent of characters. There are further corresponding shifts in the pace and subject of the verbs. The repeated use of the stately form 'era' ('there was' or 'there were'), for example, heightens the narrative and gives it a certain mysterious Biblical ring. Esteban soon becomes a mere 'human step', to which the creatures react who are now themselves the main subject ('the sea-urchin proffered its black spines, the timid oyster closed. . .'). Then by an ingenious and faintly ironic device, characteristic of Carpentier at his best, the author saves us from a surfeit of marine biology by re-introducing the young man: Esteban prises out the flesh of sea-snails with a cactus spine, the cactus leading us effort-lessly to the next internal sequence, which deals with the vegeta-tion on the cliffs rather than with the rock pools below them. (The paragraph division of the English translation has the effect of over-emphasizing this transition, which remains subtly submerged in the wholly unbroken flow of section 24 in the original). The cactus spines and thorns now do not gouge, but protect the fleshy delights of quince, melon and Indian fig, entrusted to them as guardians on the flanks of the Hesperides.

The next transition, to a level below both rock pool and cliff, is abstract and impersonal ('In contrast to this vegetation armed with spikes. . .'), but plays even more subtly with the means of the previous one. The spikes are now neither a human instrument nor a defensive armament, and recede as we all but touch the 'textures of flesh' in the coral forests, the 'yet more gorgeous countries (*paisajes*)' far below. In itself the effect is quite sugges-tive of the 'ambiguous counterpoints and rhythms' mentioned a few lines further on. For to get at this vast unarmed delight, deep in the Caribbean itself, Esteban must unarm himself in contemplation, forgoing the urge to trick his way to ravishment. As 'the man', or yet more anonymously as 'man' ('el hombre' in Spanish allows both readings), he would have to reacquire gills and scales and go back down the evolutionary scale to find a home there, 'a permanent dwelling-place' in the first luxuriance and extravagance of Creation. The closing lines, with their strong cultural and religious overtones, bring Esteban back out of his vision, leaving it as a proven experience for the meditations which fill the rest of section 24, and which culminate in the exclamation: Te Deum!

The elements of what Esteban sees are universal, like those of any vision. But their setting and configuration are specific to

Esteban's native America, to his 'Hesperides without names': his experience could not have been had by anyone anywhere. In case we have overlooked this, Carpentier reminds us later on that the beaches trodden by Esteban only then, 'three centuries after the Discovery', were beginning to have deposited on them their first pieces of polished glass: 'glass invented in Europe and strange to America'. By means of details like these, Carpentier suggests that the wonder of the American world is something unique, continental and for itself. So that Esteban's epiphany would seem to serve him principally as knowledge of a special condition. In a gesture of great boldness Carpentier would seem ideally to be distinguishing an American culture, manifest in a dazzling variety of forms traceable to the very beginning of Creation. The New World, into which the Frenchman Hugues irrupts, would then be 'other' right to its very roots.

Ideas such as these recur throughout Carpentier's mature writing and are important to the interpretation of this and of his two previous novels *The Kingdom of this World* (*El reino de este mundo*, 1949) and *The Lost Steps* (*Los pasos perdidos*, 1953). The first of these further resembles *Explosion in a Cathedral* in charting the progress of a revolution which despite European promptings assumed its own 'native' form: the uprising of the one-armed black slave Macandal (1767) which preceded Henri Christophe's successful seizure of power and the emergence of Haiti as the first Latin American state to win independence from Europe. In the prologue to *The Kingdom of this World*, Carpentier explained how he had come to write it, after an unplanned visit to Haiti in 1943. What he experienced there first converted him to his American religion: Henri Christophe's fortress La Ferrière ('a work without architectural antecedents, heralded solely by Piranesi's *Imaginary prisons*'), the dance and music of the Voodoo cult, and so on, all in intimate harmony with the strange and luxuriant flora and fauna of the place. Here, he claimed, was a spectacle of such wonder and marvel that any attempt, like his own, to describe it historically and realistically could not but produce a kind of magic. This enthusiasm was matched with strictures on the 'surrealist' writers of Europe and those Latin American writers who failed to see their own amazing surroundings properly because of their subservience to the literary fashions of Europe.

Now for Carpentier it mattered to draw distinctions of this kind, since confessedly he had himself been guilty of the sins he now condemned. As with Asturias, a Parisian education during the inter-war period (1928–39) alerted him to his own glamour as a Latin American writer, and reinforced a 'French connection' he already had via his paternal ancestry. And like Asturias's, his first published work benefits from it, his 'Afro-Cuban' novel *Ecue-yamba-O* (1933) having an exoticism akin to that of the *Legends of Guatemala*. This first novel was in fact an odd mixture of primitiv-ism and camp collage, visible in other works of the period: *Yamba O*, a 'burlesque tragedy', Paris 1928; *La passion noire*, a cantata for 10 soloists, Paris 1932, and so on. The main character in *Ecue-yamba-O*, Menegildo, scarcely exists in his own right; he appears rather as a caricature of a black America which is oppressed and at the same time exotic. As a token of his change of heart in Haiti, Carpentier vigorously disowned this early work when he became the champion of America's magic reality in all its fullness. And in the narratives of his second period, more than one charac-ter is shown to be reprehensible precisely for having sold America short, for being insensitive to its true wealth. In *The Lost Steps* a trio encountered by the hero in Venezuela is made to illustrate this failing, stereotypically: a white musicologist (a grotesque miniature of the hero),[2] an 'Indian' poet and a black painter, show themselves prepared to view the deep forests of home only from the elevation of Paris, with all its 'triviality', its freakish *actes gratuits* and artistic exploitativeness.

With its bold title, *The Kingdom of this World* succeeded in presenting American reality not as a marketable commodity but as something for itself, and announced a serious concern with origins which runs through Carpentier's subsequent writing. Yet it should be said that his censure of the European surrealists, as 'vapid necrophiliacs' 'writhing in sterile dilemma', has something decidedly bad-tempered about it. After all, both Breton, during his visit to Haiti, and Benjamin Péret (whom Carpentier knew) with his translations of Maya literature, had taken the profoundest interest in ancestral America, as indeed had Antonin Artaud during his time in Mexico. And it is not clear that their sense of 'le merveilleux', as hyperawareness of the natural world (see Breton's *L'Amour fou*), differs all that much from 'lo maravilloso' as defined by Carpentier. More seriously, for all its brilliance *The Kingdom of this World* by no means vindicates the intimate connections between natural setting and social behaviour which is made so much of in the prologue. Partly for this reason no doubt we find residues of his earlier paternalism towards indigenous and ingenuous America. Ti Noel, the black slave who witnesses Macandal's rising and execution, is better treated than Menegildo (of the disowned *Ecue-yamba-O*). But Ti Noel is not equal to the grander ambitions of the novel, and the sophistication and racial attitudes attributed to him, as Carpentier's narrative voice, are often improbable or simply insulting.

In his next novel, *The Lost Steps*, Carpentier ranged through the time and space of America more boldly and comprehensively than in any of his other works. We move from a twentieth-century English-speaking metropolis (which could be New York), through the colonial quarters of a city in Latin America (like Caracas, where he lived in the 1950s), to the stone-age life of an Indian tribe in the depths of the South American jungle (he travelled up the Orinoco while in Venezuela). These three settings are linked solely by the presence of the first-person protagonist, a professional musicologist doing field work. The 'meaning' of his journey, in larger terms, is made explicit in various ways: the presentation of each setting as a cultural moment of American history; the allotting of a special role to the woman he knows best at each stage, his actress wife, his intellectual French mistress Mouche and his stone-age lover Rosario. The novel ends by appearing to ask: 'May we retrace lost cultural steps and find our true selves?' For the moment, more important than the answer in principle is the particular route which Carpentier has mapped.

We find the thesis of *The Lost Steps*, evident enough in the novel, even more conveniently set out in Carpentier's essay 'On the marvellous reality of America' (1962; 'De lo real-maravilloso americano'),[3] which grew out of the prologue to *The Kingdom of this World*. He now turns to his continent only after engagement with such recognizably distinct world cultures as the Chinese and Islam, and thus contrives to suggest that what is true for them is true for it. In these circumstances the novel should reflect the integrity, 'lo distinto' as Carpentier puts it, of American reality in the most thorough-going fashion. In his barely-known world, his 'Hesperides without names', the novelist should indeed 'name the things' of his creation: 'just as Adam put names to the animals and plants in the Bible, so should our fiction writers baptize all that surrounds them'. He should embark on a 'journey to the seed', no less, in evolutionary terms, and retrace, as Carpentier's novel endeavours to, the 'lost steps' whereby 'style is affirmed through history'.

Such notions recall the more extreme forms of nineteenth-century evolutionary thought, in particular the kind of comprehensive 'history of Creation' (*Schöpfungsgeschichte*) elaborated by Haeckel, with his dictum 'embryology recapitulates ontology'. And in taking his argument to such lengths Carpentier does not avoid a certain philosophical awkwardness. In *The Lost Steps*, the novel of his thesis, apart from such difficulties as the fact that the hero is not an aboriginal or ancestral American, the course of the steps he takes is forever balked by the paradox of the observing consciousness (which had troubled evolutionists). The action of the hero is divorced from Carpentier's essay-like meditations, of which there are plenty, on the meaning of our backward progress in time: the narrative is either slack or simply dramatic. In contrast to Esteban who finds his way back to the first luxuriance of Creation as a lonely bather (with intuitions of having once been a fish), a 'human step', and then is again himself, the musicologist either vanishes entirely or barges his way back, set too firmly in himself for anything like the fine transitions of Esteban's exploration. Esteban literally immerses himself in his 'water-drunkenness': the musicologist, bathing naked with Rosario in an Edenic scene which has a similar function in *The Lost Steps*, can only think self-consciously, how envious people 'back there', suffocated in clothing, would be of his experience. He appears as a kind of intellectual conquistador who fails to become part of what he records, a dilemma admitted at the close of the novel perhaps, but hardly reckoned with in the main narrative.

The musicologist does not vindicate Carpentier's continental philosophy, so much as he exposes its limitations. Through him, no effective continuity can be forged, in Carpentier's own terms, between the natural and the social world. He remains an observer or an intruder, someone on or from the outside, which is where

Carpentier himself must be standing when he says in the prologue to *The Kingdom of this World*:

> And by virtue of the virginity of the landscape; of the formation, ontology and magic presence of the Indian and the negro; of the Revelation which their recent discovery entailed; and of the fertile racial mixture it propitiated, America is far from having exhausted its wealth of mythologies, What is the whole history of America but a chronicle of 'marvellous reality' ('*lo real-maravilloso*)?

Only someone essentially uninvolved in this reality could generalize about it in this fashion, equating Indian with Negro, and both, as objects of discovery, with innocent natural landscapes. In the last instance, if the musicologist represents a culture, it would be that of the Spanish conquistador. His glamour is that of the jungle adventurer, ravishing his innocent Rosario (who doesn't even have an Indian name),[4] intolerant of the insubstantiality of his enlightened French mistress Mouche, and discontent with the modern, rootless, English-speaking existence led by his wife. As with the characters in 'Journey to the Seed' ('Viaje a la semilla', completed 1944, an earlier 'evolutionist' story which also moves backwards through time to a 'primary condition'), the Discovery[5] is all-important, for before it, we are told, nothing really existed. It is as if without the very intrusion which Carpentier re-enacts in *The Lost Steps*, America would have remained unseen and uncharted, in a perpetually virginal genesis, with no true life or ontology of its own. Carpentier has censured the Americanism of novels previous to his own, from Güiraldes and Rivera to Ciro Alegría, for being too exotic, and for the falsity of what he calls their social nativism. If *The Lost Steps* differs from these precedents it is principally because of its scope and its erudition (in every sense of that word).

Carpentier's great achievement, *Explosion in a Cathedral*, carries forward but crucially modifies the enterprise of the two previous novels we have been discussing. The pages which recount Esteban's vision are among the most felicitous he has written,[6] outstanding yet not obtrusive in the novel as a whole. In this work he succeeded in using his proclivities as a writer entirely to his advantage, in a way he had not done before.

First, he condenses his evolutionist philosophy into a single crucial moment. The American genesis glimpsed in *The Kingdom of this World* and so elaborately pursued in *The Lost Steps*, is confined to the Caribbean shore, a Revelation for itself. In this smaller but teeming arena he may approach the most elemental forms, the most virgin origins. Details are observed exactly, even microscopically, and have the clean-cut quality of an engraving by Dürer, who is in fact invoked further on, in a description of dried sea urchins 'neatly arranged' like 'geometrical apples' on the sand. But here, in prose which shimmers like translucent water, we cannot precisely distinguish matter from movement, 'the inert from the palpitant'. Minute details succeed each other in slow crescendo 'with a sort of impulse springing from matter itself'. The very stones of the ocean acquire 'style and spirit'. Subject to shifts of focus and the rhythms we have noted, they partake in a process exemplified in the object which provokes Esteban's final Te Deum: the live sea-shell or caracol, which has at its core solid matter and the first turn in the spiral of life, 'the Mediator between evanescent, fugitive, lawless, measureless fluidity and the land of crystallization, structure and alternation, where everything can be grasped and weighed'. The luxury of creation witnessed by Esteban can be credibly both primeval and 'baroque', and correlate natural and cultural form. This is an intimacy explored by Carpentier in 'Journey to the Seed'[7] when he fondly hinted at the natural origins of architectural forms: 'Going against their inclination, several capitals lay in the grass. Acanthus leaves revealed their vegetable condition. A creeper ventured its tendrils towards an Ionian fluting, attracted by a feeling of familiarity'. In *Explosion in a Cathedral* the association is deeper and more comprehensive. Specialist and technical terms, which lend Carpentier's prose its 'incontrovertibility' (and which have led some[8] to bemoan his 'taxidermist' tendencies), enliven and are enlivened by their visionary context (Pythagorean, Gothic, Cambrian, weld, auriferous, counterpoint, burr, ostensory). The harmonies of this passage are subtle enough for us to be content to forget men and their actions for a while, or to see them dwarfed by their surroundings, for the Caribbean itself is here confirmed as a force in the novel, in a way that few of Carpentier's other 'settings' ever are.

Second, and more important for the novel as a whole, Carpentier works out an unprecedently rich relationship with Esteban, who is the only character who appears more or less consistently throughout the narrative. He is manipulated of course, but delicately and not at the cost either of his autonomy or of the acceptability of the 'ideas' Carpentier wants to put across, the 'philosophy' he elsewhere crams down his reader's throat. Rather, in this novel, he helps us to perceive them as something less than axiomatic and universally valid, but nonetheless inspired. Through Esteban he found a way of indulging intimate enthusiasms without being bound, as he was in *The Lost Steps*, to his American creed, with all its flaws, begged questions, convenient hiatus and covert prejudices.

Above all, Esteban is a solitary. Like Joyce's Stephen Daedalus, whose name he shares, he is ostensibly embarked on an odyssey, the voyage of Homer's epic. But his discoveries are not public. At best, as we have suggested, his American dream is opposed to the historical society activated by Hugues, from which he grows increasingly estranged and alienated. But the vision which sustains it is private, unshared and unproductive of any conceivable morality. In his 'unpeopled ocean' he is simply and ironically the 'owner' of it all. However, in a second Revelation granted to him when he goes back aboard the brig, his atavism is given a firm social shape which exists in oblique and amusing relationship with his momentary yearnings to re-acquire gills and a tail as a true denizen of the Caribbean sea.

Back aboard *L'Ami du peuple* he is asked, conveniently enough from a structural and stylistic point of view, to make an inventory of the hold. Down there the heavy smell of wine alerts him to quite another sense of his origins, as the child of the 'ancient' civilization of his Mediterranean, where

> after long being scattered, the descendants of the lost tribes had met again, to mingle their accents and their lineaments, to produce new strains, mixing and commixing, degenerating and regenerating, a temporary enlightenment followed by a leap backwards into the darkness, in an interminable proliferation of new profiles, new accents and proportions. In their turn they had been reached by the wine which had

passed from the Phoenician ships, the warehouses of Cadiz,
and the amphorae of Maarkos Sestos, into the caravels of the
Discovery, along with the guitar and the glazed tile, and
had landed on these shores so propitious to the
transcendental encounter of the Olive with the Maize.

American maize (originally a Cuban word) is allowed to be at
least nominally half of the transcendental encounter (which in
history quickly resulted in the extirpation of native Americans
from the Caribbean). But for Esteban the peoples who cultivated
it weigh little more in the balance than the non-white 'tribes' of
the Old World. There are allusions to the past proximity of the
Maya and to the vision, luminous like Esteban's, which had once
lured the Caribs up from the jungles of South America to the sea
which bears their name. But the magic blacks who had caused
such excitement when Haiti was the 'kingdom of this world'
vanish from the picture. The caracol on the shore is as it were
crushed by the caravels of Columbus's 'Discovery' (a term which
Carpentier significantly capitalizes). In this, his second search for
'style through history', so apt a sequel to the first, Esteban goes on
to remember 'with deep emotion' the old 'patriarchal' wine casks
back in the family mansion in Havana. His nostalgia is for the
well-being of a past whose style was fundamentally that of pre-
Revolutionary Europe.

It would of course be a gross mis-reading of *Explosion in a
Cathedral* to attribute Esteban's brand of Caribbean atavism
directly to his author, even if we suspect he would not find it
unattractive. For, as if to prevent this confusion, Carpentier
sometimes brings Esteban dangerously close to a political and
literary caricature. On their protector's death, for example, Esteban and his companions had been made to appear faintly ridiculous in their dread of the prospect of having to carry on the
merchandizing and trading (wine, glazed tiles?) which had kept
them in patriarchal luxury till then. By these and other means
Esteban's very propensities as a dreamer, as the visionary to whom
the deepest truths are revealed, are subtly made contingent on the
kind of character he is. For he may be discerned as a 'character'
even when saturated in his water-drunkenness. At one moment he
actively prises out tender flesh for his enjoyment with the mixture

of 'pleasure and aggression' which describes the movements of
the squadron of three lonely ships (evocative of Columbus's).
And faced with those guardian cacti he knows that to get at the
flesh and the fruit inside, to taste the 'Indian fig', the explorer he
is must 'trick' his way past the spikes, using a Spanish verb revealing the conquistador mentality: *burlar* – to ridicule, to get the
better of, to abuse. Such language recalls Carpentier's instructions to the young Latin American writer to ravish the virgin
solitudes of America, to enjoy the lush body of his continent,
leaving the stay-at-home Europeans to their necrophiliac activities,
and so on. Yet suddenly we are made aware of the dangers of
taking this conquest too far. Through Esteban's musings we learn
that anyone really anxious to enter the paradise of America, to be
truly part of 'so inaccessible' and unspoilt a Creation, and to make
it his permanent home, must revert to being a fish.

This comes almost as a sophisticated joke at the expense of
the writer who loses himself in the solitudes of America, so re-
linquishing his 'proper' place in the order of things. We discover
an effective distinction between America's 'wealth of mythologies'
and the real world, very like the one we found in Asturias. As a
would-be fish, transported by the joy of his 'ineffable vision',
Esteban bears the same relationship to Carpentier as René, the
solitary dreamer in the American wilds, bore to Chateaubriand.
Indeed, when at the end of the novel Esteban is returned, somewhat peremptorily, to his initial asthmatic condition and to suffer-
ing from a quasi-incestuous love for Sofia, he becomes the devotee
of René, 'without parents, without friends, more a solitary than
ever'. As an older man and profoundly nostalgic for the *ancien
régime*, Chateaubriand recognized that to have made his American
wilds ('les solitudes créées par moi') into his permanent home
would have meant his being 'absent from the world'.[9] By showing
Esteban up as a lonely dreamer, whose Americanism amounted
to a luxury, Carpentier offered a fine criticism of his own earlier
writing. And behind the various postures of his character he
effectively establishes a surer and less vulnerable position of his
own.

We may extend this reading of *Explosion in a Cathedral* to the
very notion of 'naming the things' of America. For as a character
Esteban appears as a near-compulsive compiler of inventories,

eminently suited to the task given him in the brig's hold. Later
in the voyage, as if dutifully naming his Hesperides he indulges
himself by inventing names for a number of curious rocks the
squadron sails past, according to fortuitous features of their
appearance (Staircase of Candles, Gorgon Island, etc). The list
can hardly be accounted more than a private toponymy of exotica,
for which however Esteban, not Carpentier, takes responsibility.

Esteban is only one of several characters in this highly complex
novel. Little attention has been paid to Hugues, the revolutionary,
or to the generous Sofia, whom some critics (including Carpentier
himself) have argued is the embodiment of a naive America which
finally asserts herself.[10] Again, Carlos and Sofia may be seen
emulating Esteban as Carpentier's literary 'agents' or accomplices.
The first is given the job of piecing together the last days of
Esteban and Sofia from fossil clues, composing a narrative within
the narrative. The second, stranded in Spain with the sickly
Esteban, constructs a Caribbean house there, and fills it with the
smells and sounds so evidently relished by the author. There is the
whole question too, of how the movement of the novel is matched
by that of other art forms, in the way that the story 'Manhunt'
('El acoso', 1956), for example, is regulated by the Eroica Sym-
phony. Epigraphs from Goya filter our experience, while the
canvas which provided the title for the English translation of the
novel, the 'apocalyptic immobilization of a catastrophe', by one
Monsu Desiderio, is brought forward at several important moments in the narrative. As a literary artifact which plays on
Carpentier's great range of professional ingenuity, this novel resists
many of the criticisms which have been levelled at him more
generally: that he views his supposed homeland in the spirit
of a Spanish conquistador, or of a French Romantic; that he
relishes Latin America for its anachronism, its underdevelopment.
Indeed, just because of the trouble that other Latin American
writers have taken to attack as well as to praise him, he has in
practice been paid the rarest honour: that of being considered a
continental point of reference.

4 *Survival in the sullied city:*

JUAN CARLOS ONETTI

He shrugged and raised his head and moved off in the direction of the unchanging sky-blue of the curtains, in the cloudy and undecided Sunday morning. He knocked on the door with the butt of his pistol and we waited for a while. The youngest girl, the round-faced blonde, slipped back a bolt and looked at us, sleepy and calm, as if she had been expecting us.

'Good morning,' she murmured towards the pistol in Marcos's hand.

We went in, blinded by the half-light, and saw in turn the tables, the pictures on the walls, the withered forgotten flowers and the hostile doors of the bedrooms. A second later we saw the man sitting at the large table in the middle, with his hat on, playing patience with greasy cards. He put the cards down on the embroidered table-cloth and greeted us matter-of-factly.

'Hello.' Larsen had his fingers interwined and wobbled his thumbs.

Marquitos went forward step by step, put the bottle on the table and started emptying his pockets.

'For the ladies,' he said.

'How kind.'

Marcos pushed the muzzle of the pistol towards the other man's face. Corpsegatherer looked at him absent-mindedly.

'I came to clean this lot up,' Marquitos explained without raising his voice. 'And personally I've nothing against you, mind. You don't exist. I'm just not keen on having a brothel in Santa Maria.'

The fattish blonde, Nelly, stood beside me, smiling at me with patience and affection.

'Would you like to sit down?' she asked me.

'No thank you. I can see better standing.'

Nelly shrugged her shoulders and went over to the table. Brushing against Marcos she picked a packet of cigarettes.

'Excuse me. You said they were for us, right?'

Marcos didn't answer her and went on playing with the gun; the woman lit a cigarette and inhaled ravenously. Then she moved away lazily and drew back a curtain. I felt that the morning light didn't suit the scene. The woman passed by me and went noiselessly into one of the bedrooms. The two men went on looking at each other; they were quite still, one standing, the other sitting; Corpsegatherer was just moving his thumbs and Marcos his pistol. After a while, evidently bored, Corpsegatherer pulled a silver watch out of his waistcoat; Marcos held the gun steady.

'Six o'clock,' Corpsegatherer said sadly. 'Just the time I was thinking of turning in. All things considered, it's one person's preference over another's.'

Marcos leant his fist on the table, spat in Corpsegatherer's face and slowly drew himself up.

'Jewish turd,' he said.

Stock-still, looking sideways at the embroidered flowers, Corpsegatherer began to smile, to rejuvenate. He seemed separate from us, from the occasion, by a long stretch of years. At last he murmured, slowly and clearly:

'Not at all one thing and hardly, they say, the other.'

Marcos let out an insulting laugh and sat down opposite Corpsegatherer. He put the pistol on the table and opened the bottle.

'There are some glasses in the cupboard,' Larsen remarked.

'Jorge,' said Marquitos.

I went up to the cupboard and hesitated for a moment. Then, smiling, I brought three glasses to the table. Marquitos glanced at me, unsure; then he filled his. Almost immediately I poured whisky into the glass I'd brought for myself and into the one I'd brought for Larsen.

'You know,' Larsen said, 'I haven't used guns for some time. Haven't carried them at least.'

The three of us drank and in the pause the voices of the women we couldn't see reached us.

'A Luger, right?' Corpsegatherer diagnosed, indicating the pistol.

Marcos filled his glass again. I couldn't see any spit on Larsen's face. One of the invisible women shouted out an order. Corpsegatherer put his empty glass to one side and moved his hand towards the pistol. Marcos watched him, unmoving, smiling contemptuously.

'Of course, a Luger,' Corpsegatherer confirmed with a happy expression. 'The best I know. Inside there's a Parabellum. Later I'll ask the girls to bring it. They're like twin sisters. But if you ask me. . .'

Polite and tactful, he put the pistol back by Marquitos's elbow. I filled up the glasses and we drank. I suddenly felt pleased and a little drunk: last night's brandy, this same night still not dead, and little sleep. Then, bustling and dressed up, gay, the women came in to welcome us.

Marcos got up and bowed, said his name and mine. He got glasses from the cupboard and handed round cigarettes. After this, smiling, forgiving, he started looking for tangos on the small white radio and danced with Maria Bonita.

And so we began to live, the six of us. I don't want to know how long we stayed together; I'm determined to forget, and do, the usual trivialities and the stupid situations. I can think we were happy to the end, when the officer and Medina knocked on the door one forgettable hour and spoke with Marcos, pretending not to see me, and handed Larsen a copy of the Governor's order.

Juntacadáveres (Montevideo 1965).
Corpsegatherer. Chapter 27.

Marcos Bergner has come to Larsen's brothel to close it and clean up the town. He has spent most of his time in the novel planning this confrontation, nurturing a bigoted hunger for violence through one drunken night to the next, until finally he grabs his gun and goes out to do the job. He is Larsen's bitterest enemy, the active expression of the outrage felt in the town, Santa Maria, that Larsen's business flourishes and was ever allowed to be set up.

Grossly offended, Larsen clearly comes out on top when at last they meet. Bergner's attack spends itself; after drinking together, he, his young companion Jorge Malabia (here the narrator) and Larsen settle down to a communal life in the brothel, with its three principal whores of unconcerned charm. In this situation they are happy (*felices*), the rarest of states for Onetti's characters; and exemplarily more successful than the six idealist 'pioneers', among them the younger Marcos Bergner, who had tried to found a 'primitive Christian' commune earlier in the novel. Larsen's is an artist's victory. As the Corpsegatherer who gives the novel its title, the collector of whores past their prime, he is masterfully cured of life's more absurd illusions. He is a kind of catcher in the sty, who has learnt to contain the most swinish assault. He is finally expelled from Santa Maria, it is true; but leaves his reign of one hundred days as a legend in the town.

For reasons that are not always convincing as narrative, Onetti delays Bergner and Larsen's crucial encounter until near the end of *Corpsegatherer*, so that the reader is the more compelled by the rush of action when it comes, by the sudden focus of nebulous and over-stretched preoccupations into sharp shapes ('with his hat on', 'greasy cards', 'small white radio'). For once independent of their author, Onetti's characters carry the fiction themselves, creating the highly-charged atmosphere and enjoining that grey unbending humour ('I can see better standing') which mark his best writing. Understanding and affecting things most is Larsen, here living his finest hour. His gestures and appearance convey matter-of-factness, faint boredom and the slightly soiled patience emblemized in his playing cards. Yet he is unbeatable and never for a moment out of control. He may not be learned in the traditional sense, but he is a connoisseur of all that pertains to his survival, guns for example. Indeed, his kin would be found less readily in consecrated literature than in the novels of Dashiel Hammett or Raymond Chandler, or in a sophisticated Western (say Spencer Tracy in *Bad Day at Black Rock*). No one could accuse Larsen of picking a fight; but his quiet self-possession and his very courtesy amount to a statement that cannot be simply ignored. And this is the source of his quasi-religious power: a spat-upon martyr who bears the initials of Jesus Christ in his sordid nickname (Junta-cadáveres).

Among the characters who recurrently inhabit Onetti's very many novels and short stories (like Gabriel García Márquez and Eduardo Mallea, he is markedly fond of genealogy and saga), Larsen is indeed privileged and long-lived. He first appeared in *No Man's Land* (*Tierra de nadie*, 1941), and displayed a resourcefulness and a fictional potential noticeable even in the crowded, fast-moving pages of that novel. As the suspect defender of a psychopathic rapist, and the acquaintance of the immoralist lawyer Aranzuru, he appears only briefly; just long enough to abduct the libidinous teenager Nora, who eventually becomes his companion in the brothel as the whore Maria Bonita. After getting permission to set up his establishment in *Corpsegatherer* his first act is to go back to Buenos Aires, to find Nora and get her help in the enterprise. As he sits at night waiting for her in the city of his youth he goes over all that had happened to him in between: his exasperated humility in a series of office jobs, his stylish contemptuousness as one of the local hard men, and his growing inner pride at his success as a pimp. This is an 'authentic' if abominable existence, which Onetti comes to endow with heavy cultural significance in this later novel. Drawing partly on the plot and the idea in the title of *No Man's Land*, he suggests that the experience of Larsen and his companions (the like of whom he had known well as a hard-headed employee of Reuters in Buenos Aires in the 1930s)[1] had been a *cosa nuestra* of some importance, a special way of life destroyed by waves of immigrants, 'Poles, Gringos, and others', who were coarser, more numerous, and finally shot their way to control of the underworld. With the murder of the 'indigenous' leader Julio, Larsen reports that everything came to an end: 'It had to be. The country (*patria*) really was finished, everything was over.'[2]

Of course Onetti is not Larsen. On the other hand the reasons for his enduring association with this character are far from casual. In the context of *Corpsegatherer*, Larsen acquires palpable historical significance, and, when expressing himself like that, responds to a question which has haunted Onetti's work more or less elusively: whether having the River Plate cities as your environment could of itself mean anything. If only because Onetti's standard answer is a bored denial that it could, and because (as Vargas Llosa has noted) he is grossly underestimated as a Latin

American writer, Larsen's explicit words about his *patria* are worth attention. Above all, Onetti is an urban writer,[3] and not given to any attempts at Romantic escape from the fact. If Larsen's commune succeeds where young Bergner's does not, it is also because the Corpsegatherer is more civilized, in his author's terms. He is a city product, 'dirty, calm and hardened', quite unlike the pure pioneers who bore each other in their isolation, victims of the simplicity they profess and of their own unknown nature. His habitat is the man-made artificial interior, preferably nocturnal, in which the morning light looks 'wrong', blue is the colour of curtains, not sky, and flowers wither and are forgotten: the very antithesis of Carpentier's marvellous America.

The epithets 'dirty, calm and hardened' are applied to the River Plate itself at the close of *No Man's Land,* as it flows past Buenos Aires in the night, observed by Aranzuru:

> There was no longer any island for sleep on on all the old earth. No friends or women for company.
>
> He heard the music of an accordion coming from the black ships by the jetty or from the bars on shore. End of the day. Unseen, at his back, was the city with its dirty air and the tall buildings, with the coming and going of people, hellos, death, hands and faces, games. It was night already and the city hummed under the lights, with its men, its hats, children, handkerchieves, shop-windows, steps, steps like blood, like hail, steps like an aimless current.
>
> Here, he was sitting on a stone, with the last stain of a seagull in the air and the oil stain on the dirty, calm, hardened river.

The city is registered here, as a precondition of any imaginable life, in a way which from the start precludes enthusiasm for the New World and naive faith in its 'magic'. The river flowing by is irreversibly remote from any natural source, from the 'blooming wilds' and 'worlds of solitude' upstream. Natural America is not just overlooked but positively transmuted into the social, sordid, deprived and anonymous: a secondary, unvirgin state.

When the characters in *No Man's Land* are themselves led to ask where it is that they live, they can find only oblique answers.

To this extent the title is literal. And inset into the narrative are factual reminders of its meaning: quoted advertisements, for example, like: BRISTOL – IMPORTED CIGARETTES (tobacco is after all an American plant). Coming from a part of Latin America that knew industrialization early, and has strong connections with the commercial West, Onetti is indicating where not to look for identity. Hence his impatience with those who can only extol the beauty of natural landscapes like the pampa and hold up an 'indigenous' American figure like the gaucho as one relevant to modern times. This kind of response is no less a 'farce', he says, than dealing in straight pre-Columbiana (the Indians of the pampas suffered a fate as catastrophic as those of the Great Plains, at the same period and for similar reasons). Onetti suspects that his part of the New World at least is without roots and prematurely senile. No claim it might have to being 'different' can ignore this fact. And Larsen does not. As one who has seen the 'real' Buenos Aires fall from its fortune in history he holds in himself the special truth of his *patria*; the glittering nostalgia of Gardel[4] and the tango; an aggressive contempt for naiveté in any form; and the xenophobia of one who bears his own rootlessness in his name (as does Onetti, once O'Nety). But this is a fragile almost secret truth, to be guarded closely and shared, laconically, only with those also able to understand.

By making Larsen revisit Buenos Aires and fetch Nora in *Corpsegatherer*, Onetti integrates a latent historical questioning of his, or the residue of it, with what had in the meantime become his principal occupation as a writer: the creation and peopling of Santa Maria, the coastal 'somewhere' in Entre-Rios or Corrientes where the brothel is finally established. In one of his best novels, *Brief Life* (*La vida breve*, 1950),[5] the reader witnesses the extraordinary birth of this town, a kind of River Plate Yoknapatawpha (Faulkner being important in many ways for Onetti).[6] Juan Maria Brausen, a character in the novel who is bored with his trivial job and as incapable of further feeling for his wife as he is of forgetting her, escapes his condition by dreaming up fellow characters: a certain doctor Díaz Grey, a 'fictional' Brausen, and Onetti himself. These characters then struggle between themselves for psychic supremacy in the novel. Gradually Díaz Grey predominates and becomes the guide to yet further characters who find a point of reference in his consciousness and then in the houses and streets of Santa Maria itself.

In the many books of Onetti's Santa Maria saga, Grey often acts as an authorial confessor. It is he who records the spoilt lives, the petty betrayals and inadmissible neuroses of the principal family in the town: Jorge Malabia's sick love for his sister-in-law Julita, the prurient hypocrisy of her brother-in-law Marcos Bergner, and so on. *For a Nameless Tomb* (*Para una tumba sin nombre*, 1959), for example, is the story of Rita, a maid seduced and abandoned by Marcos and then exploited as a prostitute by Jorge. Díaz Grey's judgment is implicit, but never simple and always evanescent; Onetti's hypersensitivity to the idea of misrepresentation and to confession as an irrevocable lapse means that reported acts themselves can abruptly be suggested to have been illusory. In *Brief Life* and *For a Nameless Tomb*, Onetti deals through Dr Grey with obessions in terms less disheartening than those of the Freudian analysis they would seem to invite and which he expressly abhors; obsessions announced already in his first work *The Well* (*El pozo*, 1939), an aggressively 'anti-literary' narrative spoken by a first person who is both adolescent and acutely critical of the value of his incessant fantasies.[7] Elsewhere, Díaz Grey acts as little more than a fixture in the given setting of Santa Maria. This is especially true of the stories which deal with people further from the structural centre of the town; visitors living on the outskirts, like the incestuous athlete in *The Goodbyes* (*Los adioses*, 1954), or the reporter in 'Hell So Feared' (*El infierno tan temido*, 1962), who is driven to suicide by his ex-wife's practice of sending him obscene photographs of herself.

Onetti first brought Larsen to Santa Maria when he began writing *Corpsegatherer*. However, before finishing and publishing this novel he produced another, also about Larsen in Santa Maria, which in many respects is better. Onetti reports that he could not rid himself of a sudden vision of Larsen's final demise, which is the subject of *The Shipyard* (*El astillero*, 1961). Characteristically aware of the absurdity of the act, Larsen returns to Santa Maria after his expulsion as a brothel-owner (which however had not yet been fully related since *Corpsegatherer* remained to be finished), to become the employee of Petrus, an erstwhile shipping magnate. The business is in irremediable decline: machinery stands idle and rusts, the two remaining clerks ritually handle correspondence from years back. Larsen goes into all this as a new manager, playing the game harder than they, and ostensibly works to get things going again. He even courts Petrus's stupid daughter, furthering an ambition appropriate to his position in the firm. His unpardonable mistake, according to his own in-grained code, is to believe fleetingly that his adopted system has meaning and purpose, to fancy in an unguarded moment that his existence might have acquired hope and hence honour. This offence precipitates his definitive end. The passages in which Larsen realizes this is so are among Onetti's best. Details of season, place and character cohere in a remarkably single-minded ex-istential statement. Haunted by the 'impure hatred' from the past of men and women whom he has deceived, he bears himself through grey wet winter, consulting Dr Grey, diagnoser of pal-pable ill-health, and serving the respected Petrus, who turns out to be a cheat, and an inept one at that. He strays through junk-strewn yards, oppressed by the decaying machinery, recognizing the obsolete bureaucracy of the firm as a mode of comfortably evading a grotesquely hopeless state of affairs. One of his very last acts is to make love to the maid backstairs in the gentleman Petrus's villa; a sad echo of his old underworld self, too muted now to be in any way subversive.

Devoting this whole book to a character who was congenial to him, Onetti plumbs the lower depths of a misanthropy which verges on pessimism. Always avoiding the temptation to shrill directness (the chapters are carefully disposed and titled like scenes from a play) no less than social or psychological 'explana-tion', Onetti performs an exorcism, notably as Larsen catches the southern spring with his dying breath, in a paragraph at the end of *The Shipyard*, its lyricism enclosed within parentheses:

> (. . .As the launch shook with its engines, Larsen, covered by the dry sacks they had thrown over him, could imagine in detail the destruction of the shipyard buildings could hear the wheezing of ruin and decay. But the hardest bit to take must have been the unmistakable, capricious breeze of September, the first thin smell of spring slipping through the chinks of decrepit winter. He breathed it as the launch beat

its way upstream. He died of pneumonia in Rosario before the week was out, and in the hospital's papers there is a full record of his real name.)

Onetti confesses that it was hard, tantamount to an exhumation, to return to the script of *Corpsegatherer* after this exhaustive exercise. The novel lacks the drive of *The Shipyard*. Larsen seems out of place 'after' his journey to death, after facing walls infinitely more blank than those of Santa Maria's self-righteous inhabitants. Apart, possibly, from Bergner, his opponents appear provincial, even folkloric, and at moments the action degenerates into a farce no amount of heavy irony can redeem. Correspondingly, Díaz Grey relapses into a role less pertinent, more obtrusively omniscient, than in *The Shipyard*. And certain chapters have prompted charges of self-plagarism, or of simply bundling together previously untold episodes of the Santa Maria saga.[8] But Onetti's most genial invention, the character Larsen, cured of life's illusions, even of life itself, reveals yet further strengths, risen now from his very grave.

After such professionally Latin American novelists as Asturias and Carpentier, Onetti comes over to us in a different way. He shares none of their enthusiasms for the idea of America as a strange or magic extant reality. Moreover, as an urban novelist who is beyond all that, he reminds us continuously that the settings and characters in his novels (after *No Man's Land*) are quite imaginary, barely-disguised figments of a mind primarily concerned with universal problems of an existential and even a theological nature. In this he no doubt resembles many other major River Plate writers, among them Macedonio Fernández, Ernesto Sábato and of course Borges. What distinguishes him however, and explains the keen interest of fellow novelists in his work, is his ability to 'precipitate' a minimal but substantial reality in his novels, which is unapologized for and unenhanced by inherited literary and other myths. For all Onetti's corrosive scepticism and the apparent reluctance with which he establishes a setting or grants autonomy to his characters, the atmosphere and style of moments like Bergner's encounter with Larsen have a quite dazzling immediacy of their own. The merest turn of speech, the smallest material object, are given and arranged by one wholly intimate with them, so that barely noticed they generate their own atmosphere. By the time Bergner looks for tangos on Larsen's small white radio we are tuned in to a quite particular time and place. And this is an antipodal redoubt where, we are reminded with urbane and stoic resentment, it is September that announces spring, the season of Larsen's death.

Province of dead souls:

JUAN RULFO

Noises. Voices. Murmurs. Distant songs:
>   *My girl gave me a handkerchief*
>   *with a hem of weeping. . .*
Falsetto. As if the people singing were women.

I saw the carts go by. The oxen moving slowly. The creaking of the stones under the wheels. The men looking as though they were still asleep.

'. . .*Early every morning the village shakes as the carts go by. They come from all around, heaped up with salt-lick, maize cobs, para grass. The wheels squeak making the windows vibrate, waking people up. It's at this time of day that the ovens are opened and it smells of newly-baked bread. And the sky may suddenly fill with thunder. The rain may fall. Spring must be near. There you will get used to the cloudbursts, my son.*'

Empty carts, grinding the silence of the streets. Vanishing on the dark road of night. And the shadows. The echo of the shadows.

I made up my mind to go back. Up above me I felt the track I had come along like an open wound in the blackness of the hills.

Then someone touched me on the shoulder.

'What are you doing here?'

'I came to look for. . .,' and I was just about to say whom when I checked myself: 'I came to look for my father.'

'Why don't you come in?'

I went in. It was a house with half the roof fallen in. The tiles on the floor. The roof on the floor. And in the other half a man and a woman.

'Aren't you dead?' I asked them.

And the woman smiled. The man looked at me seriously.

'He's drunk,' said the man.

'He's just startled,' said the woman.

There was a paraffin stove. There was a canvas bed, and a chair with her clothes on it. Because she was naked, as God cast her into the world. And he too.

'We heard someone moaning and knocking his head against our door. And there you were. What's been happening to you?'

'So many things have happened to me that I'd most like to sleep.'

'We were already asleep.'

'Let's sleep then.'

Pedro Páramo (Mexico 1955),
pages 50–1

The person talking is the legitimate but unacknowledged son of the man after whom this novel of Rulfo's is named: Pedro Páramo. His own name (which is not revealed straight away) is Juan Preciado and he inherits it from his mother Dolores. It is she who urges him, on her death, to go to her old village, Comala, to find his father and avenge himself and her for the bad life Pedro Páramo has made for them. Her last conversations with Juan come back to him insistently, like her memories of the village as it used to be, in italicized fragments like the one above. The contrast between that lost springtime and the atmosphere Juan encounters could not be greater, and Rulfo reiterates it liturgically.

Juan's actual entry into ghostly Comala, with its half-heard, half-anonymous 'noises, voices and murmurs' is skilfully narrated. His first words in the novel show that he is already there ('I came to Comala to look for my father'). Sure details of his arrival and of any place he came from can be only fragmentarily put together. Only vague information can be gleaned from his mother's last instructions, or from his exchange with the carter (whose name we never know) who shows him the road. The same obscurity surrounds the object of his search. Answers to his questions come piecemeal and evasively from informants who themselves have nebulous identity. For many pages we know little more than what the carter says, that Pedro Páramo is 'living rancour', ('un rencor vivo'). Only when Juan gives up his endeavour and dies 'into' the village about half-way through the book does the whole story begin to come out. Then Pedro Páramo emerges as a brutal greedy man, a cacique or local potentate[1] who murdered repeatedly to gain more land, aided by his crooked lawyer; who abused countless women, aided by an abject procuress; who maims out of insane jealousy and betrays his closest allies without a twinge of guilt, and who possesses a Darwinian instinct for political survival during the upheavals of the Mexican Revolution. His only reason for marrying Dolores Preciado, Juan's mother, had been to acquire her large estate. The only son he recognizes, not hers and illegitimate, is one closest to him in depravation, Miguel. But he is by no means a caricature: some of the most intensely lyrical passages in the novel reveal his tenderness for the lovely Susana San Juan, who rejects him, and for his son Miguel. Rather, such love as he is shown to be capable of feeling is manically limited to the very few he favours, and whose lives he spoils as much as anyone else's. His last act is his grandest. To settle an imagined affront he decides to starve Comala to death, and does so. His enduring rancour populates the village with 'sombras', shadows in the half-light, and the shades of people only half-alive, and reduces the countryside to the arid plain (*páramo*) of his own name.

While Juan Preciado enters the novel as a more or less defined character, his identity derives from little more than his reason for going to Comala, and his mother's pervasive, lyric memory. He reports few of his thoughts beyond the repeated, and never achieved, desire 'to go back'. As he wanders from ruin to ruin through weed-covered streets his 'encounters' with others are always oblique and never full enough to reassure him even of his own continuing existence. When he thinks of going back, of recovering a notional past of his own, a hand will touch him on the shoulder, or a voice from nowhere will invite him to come in, to penetrate further. In this way he becomes absorbed by Comala, and copes as an individual ever less easily with his situation. Voices, which are echoes 'locked in the hollowness of the walls or under the stones', and which 'tread on his heels', threaten increasingly to make him no more than one of themselves, they in turn being destined to fade altogether one day. His presence becomes less substantial than the disembodied dialogues which make up most of the book and which Rulfo composes with such evident mastery.

By the time Juan Preciado enters the half-ruined house of the naked couple, he is nearing the end of his existential tether. Before long he is incorporated into their company, his last, to the extent of taking the man's place; the man is the woman's brother and soon abandons the house on an obvious pretext. Finally Juan sleeps with the woman; a suffocating encounter with unredeemed clay, and for him, ultimate knowledge. 'That woman's body made of clay, caked with clay, fell apart as if it was dissolving into a pool of mud. I felt myself swimming in the sweat which poured off her, deprived of the air you need to breathe.' He goes out into the street to find relief, but finds none: 'I had to inhale the same air that left my mouth.' Anagnorisis is complete; he has come home to expire.

> I recall having seen something like foaming clouds whirling above my head and then drenching myself in that foam and being lost in its cloud. It was the last thing I saw.

From this moment on his grammatical first person vanishes from the narrative and joins the collective unconscious. The awareness of Comala as a situation, which Juan Preciado had provided as a narrative thread, becomes the more immediate responsibility of the author, who now orchestrates the voices of the village, including Juan's to tell less elusively the tale of the bad-man Pedro Páramo. And as we hear Juan's voice emerging from a grave next to that of Dorotea, Pedro Paramo's old procuress, with Susana San Juan lying restlessly a little further off, we are faced with the disconcerting possibility that he may have been dead all along.

Once in Comala Juan Preciado can find no escape, being drawn to an ineffectual end which no amount of will or imagination can avert. For the ghosts are stronger than he, paradoxically solider, more earthy. His very appearance makes them think he is odd, 'drunk' or 'startled'. They disregard him as a casual event, a kind of soothsayer endowed perhaps with larger awareness of their general predicament, but by that very token more vulnerable, like a certain 'prophet' from Media Luna for example, who proved unable to prophesy that the local *patrón* would do him in.

The ghostly voices around him permeate his being and still him. His psychic independence and his flesh alike are sapped by his surroundings, drained to the end. His search is stopped by the stasis of the village, the dazzling immobility of the *capitana* grass on the cobbled streets, the dusty smell of decay in the woman's bed ('como de orines'), the pillow stiff with old sweat, the jagged hole in the roof against the sky. Up above he may see clouds and birds move untrammelled, though even the birds must hurry before the dark 'closes their roads' as it closes his own track in the hills. He is held by the atmosphere of Comala, in its voices, shapes and smells, without escape. The movement of time itself relentlessly solidifies into the place which confines him.

With its atmosphere of suffocation and abandonment, Comala stands as the heritage of rural Mexicans whom Rulfo has known and spent many years of his life with.[2] The paternal gift that is Pedro Páramo's to Juan, was first made with the arrival of Cortes and the conquistadors, who brought the title 'Don' that Páramo so insists on, and the fiery stallion ridden by his pathological son Miguel. These were the men who felled the forests and killed the birds of Mexico, purposefully to make a desert, a *páramo*, which would remind them of the eroded landscape of home; who devastated the habitat of the women they allotted themselves with the same callousness with which Pedro Páramo takes his 'fistfuls of flesh'. They have been there too long to be resented simply as intruders (as, for example, Asturias's *maiceros* and *ladinos* are), or even to be conceptualized as such. That is part of Juan's problem as the 'avenger' of his mother Dolores, one of Páramo's victims. The commingling of 'cultures' has reached the point of incest, so that as a glimpse of fresh innocence Dolores is anomalous (as she is also naive and defenceless, being only too easily exploited and appropriated with her estate). Juan's task is hopeless from the start; penetration has been too deep.

The only apparent survivors of this historical catastrophe are the Indians, who later on come down from the hills with their herbs in the rain, laughing and joking amongst themselves. The freshness around them may be reminiscent of Dolores's memories, of the spring rain and the fat maize cobs recalled in turn by Juan. But Rulfo certainly does not encourage us to associate her with them, to politicize in this way. His Indians are decidedly less accessible than Altamirano's Nicolás, or than those of the artists of the Mexican Revolution. In Diego Rivera's murals, for example, Mexican Indians are depicted as the first principle of nationhood; and Gregorio López y Fuentes's novel *El indio* (1935) proposes them as a social model.[3] The Indians in *Pedro Páramo* are by definition intact, beyond reach, and therefore cannot be party to Dolores's intuitions of a lost Mexican Eden. Significantly enough, these memories of hers fade entirely from the text as soon as her son 'dies' and meets his true inheritance in Comala.

The Church, the traditional source of redemption in Mexico since the traumatic arrival of Pedro Páramo's ancestors from Spain, cannot help his descendants and victims any more than the Indians in the hills can. Centuries of abuse have killed whatever virtue that institution had, so that it is no longer in the power of a rural priest to absolve even when he wants to. The spiritual guardian of Comala, Father Renteria, has so compromised himself, so consented to the evil committed by Pedro Páramo and the depraved Miguel, that he can no longer help his flock. They have all fallen from grace and live in a Dantesque purgatory with oblivion as their only future. Indeed, as Joseph Sommers has pointed out, the 'very substance' of *Pedro Páramo* is the pagan belief of Mexican folklore in 'ánimas en pena', souls condemned and unabsolved, who wander the earth bodiless, and overcome the living.[4] One of the most explicit passages in the novel is the upbraiding Renteria receives from the diocesan authority at Contla. The problems of 'poor villages' like Comala are presented here from the outside as nowhere else in the novel. As overt political comment, this passage exposes the rawness of Rulfo's own anger at the peasants' dependence on an authority which has cynically persisted in appeasing their worst oppressors.

As an intimate of a forlorn American hinterland which holds neither glamour nor mystery, Juan Rulfo, in his one novel and his single short-story collection *The Burning Plain* (*El llano en llamas*, 1953), may well be compared to Graciliano Ramos, one of the authors of the Brazilian North East. His *Barren Lives* (*Vidas secas*, 1938) conveys a sense of utter erosion by means startlingly similar to Rulfo's. He, too, familiarizes us with the basic conditions of his region by returning to the same undeniable events from more than one point of view and by dwelling on its unavoidable truths. Colours especially acquire the same elemental intensity they do with Rulfo, even to the point of detail: 'the pure bad blue of the sky'; 'the blackness of the hills'; 'the blackness of the vultures' are phrases taken from one or other book. In both novels yellow also has an elemental function, as the baleful colour of a policeman's uniform (Ramos) and a sinister bad smell (Rulfo); and the lush green paradise of Dolores evokes the one dreamt of by Ramos's character Fabiano. But we also find a crucial and most instructive difference. For Ramos does not leave the poor man of his landscape totally without hope, sucked dry as he is by his environment and his exploiters. At the end of *Barren Lives*, Fabiano gives up and goes 'back' to the town where there is a possible forum for the kind of revolutionary change Ramos believed was necessary in Brazil.[5] Juan Preciado is not left even with that remote hope, simply because Mexico is supposed to have had its revolution already. Indeed, the failure of successive Mexican governments to put their revolutionary programmes into practice in the countryside is for Rulfo a profounder reason for anger than the weakness of the Church.

This is shown well in his short story 'They gave us the land', ('Nos han dado tierra')[6] which records the thoughts and conversations of a group of peasants walking over the lot apportioned to them as a result of the government's redistribution of property. The piece of plain in question is so 'hard and eroded' as to be unploughable, a point which a delegate they meet asks them to put in writing before he disappears. The hopeless lack of understanding between the politicians, good or bad, and the rural communities of Mexico (examined again recently in Gleizer's film *The Frozen Revolution*) is the bitter source of other stories in *The Burning Plain*. In the novel, *Pedro Páramo*, Mexico's revolution could hardly be presented more disenchantedly. Even during the early heroic days Páramo, the landowner, survives its challenge without too much difficulty, turning to his own advantage the ignorance and the blood-lust of the leaders and the troops who arrive, exploiting their ill-defined and shifting loyalties. They are shown as supporters now of Villa, then of Carranza, next of the Catholic Counter-Revolutionaries, in a tautly narrated confusion reminiscent of Mariano Azuela's despairing chronicle of the decade

1910–20, *The Underdogs* (*Los de abajo*, 1915), which however does not expose why rural Mexicans behave as they do. Platoons and ideologies pass through and by Comala, too little connected with it in any way to change the atmosphere which suffocates Juan Preciado.

The body of literature about the Mexican Revolution is of course formidably large. Foreign writers like D. H. Lawrence, Graham Greene, Antonin Artaud, Malcom Lowry[7] have responded strongly to it, each in his own way. In Mexican literature the line stretches from Azuela's *The Underdogs*,[8] to novels like Fuentes's *The Death of Artemio Cruz* (*La muerte de Artemio Cruz*, 1962), which registers the corruption of the revolutionary leader Cruz by ideologically hostile forces, above all those of U.S. capitalism, and to Octavio Paz's famous essay *Labyrinth of Solitude* (*El laberinto de la soledad*), which traces certain psychological patterns back to the trauma of the Conquest and to pre-Columbian times. Rulfo is apparently less ambitious than this, and indeed would not disown the epithet provincial. This is precisely the source of his strength. He stems from the dry southern part of Jalisco. But we need no map to locate Comala. He no more chronicles the peculiarities of his region, unlike Agustín Yáñez, for example (whose chronicles of revolutionary Mexico are very much 'set' in the more fertile north of the same province), than he diagnoses national problems on the grand scale of Fuentes or Paz. If we want analogues for Rulfo's achievement they would sooner be found among the novelists of 'marginal', isolated communities further afield with whom he has expressed sympathy: the French-Swiss Ramuz, the Icelander Halldor Laxness and certain Scandinavians including Onetti's early model Knut Hamsun. This firm preference of his, which contrasts as if purposefully with that of many 'mainstream' Latin American authors, has in it an implicit comment of its own which some of those authors, among them Paz, have not always found to their liking.[9]

Rulfo is immersed in provincial Mexico to the point of ultimate recognition. He is superlatively aware of how hard it is to preserve a moral or even psychic independence in that world, of the kind which guarantees Juan Preciado's individuality at least for a time (though Juan ventures no overt comments of his own), or which those anonymous 'soothsayers' have who come to a bad end. In these circumstances, rather than enforce a strong narrative line, Rulfo relies on conversation and spoken thoughts, turns of phrase which he has learned to translate and arrange with a skill comparable to Onetti's, dialogue being a supreme test. Without recourse to dialect or regional expression, Rulfo finds a mode of speech which is local, integral with its landscape. He operates more with cadence and syntax than lexically. There is a kind of grim disheartenedness in what Juan Preciado and the inhabitants of Comala say which stems partly from their refusal to conjoin or erect structures grammatically, and partly from the withdrawal implicit in their use of the undefined 'they', impersonal and modified personal particles, and in their preferring the accusative to the nominative first person (incidentally a feature of certain Mexican Indian languages). 'I came to Comala because they told me my father lived here, a certain Pedro Páramo. My mother told me.' The resignation exuded already in these opening phrases grows steadily through the book to the point of hypnosis. The closest thing in Spanish to the speech of Comala's inhabitants are the recordings made by anthropologists among rural Mexicans (including the remarkable autobiography of a Maya Indian from Chiapas, *Juan Pérez Jolote*,[10] published three years before *Pedro Páramo*), familiar to Rulfo in his capacity as director of the editorial department of the National Indigenist Institute. In his novel he so orchestrates their voices that their collective effect is to render precarious any consciousness other than their own.

The degree to which Rulfo's characters persuade is well brought out in a short story which anticipated the end of *Pedro Páramo* in many respects. This is the story of Juvencio Nava, who has been brought in for murder committed many years before; it is called by the words he insistently repeats, 'Tell them not to kill me!' ('¡Díles que no me maten!') and told mostly through his spoken thoughts and exchanges with his son. The atmosphere Rulfo evokes from the smell of the road ('como de orines', like Juan Preciado's last bed) and the shadows on it, is so convincingly shaped by Nava's speech that the reader comes to accept it like a code, and feels neither indulgent towards him as a doomed man, pathetic as he is, nor outraged by the murder he has committed, hideous as it was. In this way we become attuned even to the grim humour of the son after Nava's summary execution: he brings his father home, telling the corpse how odd the family will find his face, deprived by gunshots of the last vestiges of human form. Nava is made 'inhuman' and yet familiar, like Pedro Páramo himself by the time he slumps to the ground 'like a heap of stones' at the end of the novel. Bad as he is, he inspires neither revulsion nor sympathy within his world, which Rulfo makes his reader share; and the last justice administered on him by the drunken Don Abundio is as unhelpful as that received by Nava.

According to Rulfo the would-be reformer of this situation should move warily and has a lot to learn. In such ruins of 'living rancour' and such 'natural' vindictiveness the true and successful avenger of Dolores Preciado will be hard to find. On the other hand, whatever their interest in Latin America, anyone who reads Rulfo carefully cannot fail to recognize the quality of his witness.

'Wait a minute,' Traveler said doubtfully. 'Can't you hand him the package from there?'

'Of course she can't,' Oliveira said, surprised. 'What's on your mind? You're ruining everything.'

'Like he says, I can't hand it to him from here,' Talita admitted, 'but I could toss it, the easiest thing in the world from here.'

'Toss it?' Oliveira said resentfully. 'All this trouble and you're going to end up by tossing me the package?'

'If you stick out your arm you'll only be a foot away from the package,' Traveler said. 'There's no need for Talita to go all the way over there. She'll toss you the package and that's that.'

'She'll miss, the way women always do,' Oliveira said, 'and the *yerba* will spill all over the street, not to mention the nails.'

'Rest assured,' Talita said, quickly taking out the package. 'Even if it doesn't land in your hand, it will still go through the window.'

'Yes, and it'll spill all over the dirty floor and I'll have to drink *maté* that's all full of dust,' Oliveira said.

'Don't pay any attention to him,' Traveler said. 'Go ahead and throw it and come on back.'

Talita turned around to look at him, doubting whether he meant what he was saying. Traveler was looking at her in a way that she knew very well, and Talita felt a sort of caress run up over her shoulder. She clutched the package and gauged the distance.

Oliveira had lowered his arms and seemed indifferent to what Talita was or was not going to do. He was looking at Traveler over Talita's head, and Traveler returned his look fixedly. 'Those two have got another bridge stretched between them,' Talita thought. 'If I were to fall into the street they wouldn't even notice it.' She looked down at the cobblestones, she saw the errand-girl looking up at her with her mouth open; two blocks away she saw a woman coming along who must have been Gekrepten. Talita paused with the package resting on the bridge.

'That's the way it is,' Oliveira said. 'It had to happen, nobody can change you. You come right up to the edge of things and one gets the idea that finally you're going to understand, but it's useless, you see, you start turning them around to read the labels. You always get stuck in the planning stage, man.'

'So what?' Traveler said. 'Why do I have to play games with you, chum?'

'Games play along all by themselves; you're the one who sticks a pole in the spokes to slow down a wheel.'

'A wheel that you invented, if you want to bring that up.'

'I don't agree,' Oliveira said. 'All I did was create the circumstances, as anyone who can understand would see. The game has got to be played clean.'

'You sound like a loser, old man.'

'It's easy to lose if the other man is rolling the dice.'

'Big shot,' Traveler said. 'Real gaucho talk.'

Talita knew that somehow they were talking about her, and she kept on looking down at the errand-girl, motionless on her chair with her mouth open. 'I'd give anything for them to stop arguing,' Talita thought. 'No matter what they talk about, it's always about me in the end, but that's not what I really mean, still it's almost what I mean.' It had occurred to her that it would be very funny to drop the package so that it would fall into the errand-girl's mouth. But she didn't really think it would be funny because she could feel that other bridge stretched out above her, the words that passed back and forth, the laughs, the hot silences.

'It's like a trial,' Talita thought. 'Like a ritual.'

She recognized Gekrepten, who had reached the next corner and was beginning to look up. 'Who's judging you?'

Oliveira had just said. But it wasn't Traveler they were judging, it was she. A feeling, something sticky, like the sun on the back of her neck and on her legs. She was going to have an attack of sunstroke, that's what the punishment would probably be. 'I don't think you're in any position to judge me,' Manú had said. Still it wasn't Manú but she who was being judged. And through her God knows what, while stupid Gekrepten was waving her left arm around and making motions as if she was the one who was about to have an attack of sunstroke and fall down into the street, condemned without appeal.

Rayuela (Buenos Aires 1963). Translated by Gregory Rabassa as *Hopscotch* (London 1967). Chapter 41.

The 'bridge' Talita is perched on stretches across a Buenos Aires street from her husband Manú or Traveler's room to Oliveira's. It has been improvised from two planks, weighted at their respective ends by a wardrobe and other items of furniture and bound together in the middle by rope; Talita is hot and uncomfortable, and gets dizzy from time to time looking down at the street below, at the errand-girl on her chair, open-mouthed and thirsty for blood. She comes to find herself up there because of Horacio Oliveira's desire to have some straight shiny nails (for purposes unknown) and some herbs to brew some *maté* with. The journey down two flights of stairs, across the street and up another two and back was rejected as too strenuous for the heat of that afternoon, and in the end he manages to have his supplies brought across in a packet by Talita. Hence the accusation by Traveler that Oliveira started it all ('a wheel that you invented'). Oliveira's response, that he merely 'created the circumstances', goes beyond self-defence to intimate a quality in the situation finally made explicit by Talita when she says it reminds her of a 'trial' or a 'ritual'. The scene as a whole is one of the longest and most brilliant in Cortázar's novel *Hopscotch*, one in which he felt that as author he had come closest to enhancing meaning with the humour of Jarry, to revealing destinies in a game or a joke.

If any destiny is being decided on this occasion it is Oliveira's. He is deep in an encounter on which his life, such as it is, hinges. As Talita is aware, he and Traveler are talking about her: at one level the ceremony is about whether Talita will stay over on Oliveira's side or whether she will return to her husband. Oliveira is angry because Traveler isn't playing fair: he has looked at Talita in a private way 'she knew very well' and which she felt as a caress. Oliveira's first reaction is to appear 'indifferent', but then he accuses Traveler of putting a spoke in the wheels, of not letting the game 'play itself'. His own way of playing clean is to refrain from this kind of direct appeal and not to force the situation. If he woos Talita then it is within a convention which is decorously abstract and which generates its own dialectics, in this case that of one of their fabulous 'seesaw-question' games. While Traveler is looking for a hat for Talita and is temporarily absent from his end of the bridge, they launch into such an exchange. Perhaps Oliveira's least guarded enthusiasm and warmest courtship come in his response to one of Talita's efforts in their dialogue, which in addition is set off against the dull predictability of Gekrepten's report on her afternoon's doings.

> 'I remember one now,' Talita said.
> 'And what do you think happened,' Gekrepten said. 'I get to the dentist's, on the Calle Warnes. I ring the bell, and the receptionist comes to the door. I say: "Good afternoon." She says: "Good afternoon. Please come in." I come in and she takes me into the waiting room.'
> 'It's like this,' Talita said. 'One whose cheeks are puffed up, or a row of buckets lashed together and floated like a raft to a place where reeds grow: a storehouse for items of prime necessity, established so that certain persons can acquire them there more economically than in a store, and everything pertaining to or relative to the eclogue, isn't it like applying the science of galvanism to a living or dead animal?'
> 'Such beauty,' Oliveira said astounded. 'It's simply phenomenal.'
> 'She tells me: "Please sit down for a moment." And I sit and wait.'

By 'dazzling' Oliveira, Talita becomes so much more like La Maga, the woman he had loved in Paris, the mother of a dead child Rocamadour, who works magic (as her name suggests she should), less articulately but no less powerfully than Talita. Oliveira's 'indifference' to what Talita 'was or was not going to do' is surely feigned; he is increasingly obsessed by her and he ends by identifying her wholly with La Maga. Finally he declares himself by kissing her in the refrigeration room of the psychiatric clinic that they and Traveler work in (another crucial act counterposed to its setting). This 'give-away' gesture leads to remorse, paranoia and Oliveira's probable end, a breach in the strict code he has accused Traveler of infringing (when he said: 'It's easy to lose if the other man is rolling the dice.').

Traveler's response to this stricture in the plank scene is undermined, as a concession, by irony: 'Big shot. Real gaucho talk.' He implies that games with the sheep-bone die (*taba*) typical of the Argentine gaucho, are not to the point. But as the more gaucho, or at least the more national of the two, the owner of the solider plank and a surer 'home', the husband of Talita at this point gives ground to Oliveira. Though Talita finally inches her way back to him, and though his irony finally beats Oliveira's brilliance, he yields weight to the other half of their dual identity in the dialectic they themselves generate. For as Talita is well aware, 'those two have got another bridge stretched between them' above the one she is on, and more important than it. Indeed, in one of his strategies, Oliveira has insisted on their similarities in order to discover the differences between them; he says to Talita: 'Two blokes with black hair, with the faces of Buenos Aires toughs, with the same scorn for almost the same things. . .'. Away in Paris, 'on the other side', Oliveira had thought hard about his capacity for self-transcendence, for moving out of his square in the hopscotch game, and had recognized among other things, 'that he was middle-class, he was *porteño* [from Buenos Aires], that he was Colegio Nacional, and that you can never do anything about those things'. At the same time he had recognized Traveler as his *Doppelgänger* in distant Buenos Aires, which is 'this side' in Cortázar's description: his other half whom he could have been or could be. Hence the intensity of their reciprocal gaze over Talita's head.

Encounters of this kind abound in Cortázar's work and patently derive from the oriental philosophers, when not from Borges. We may detect, too, echoes of Robbe-Grillet and the French *nouveau roman*. In an early short story in *End of the Game* (*Final del juego*, 1956), the narrator is mysteriously drawn to contemplate an axolotl, an American amphibian (which by the way is essentially and etymologically 'two lived' in Nahuatl literature). He feels his mind being gradually transferred to the other side of the glass which he presses his head against, until it is clear that he has actually become the axolotl. Metempsychosis is also at the root of 'The Island at Midday' ('La isla a mediodía'); an airline steward staring at the island below through the glass porthole imagines another life down there with such intensity that for narrative purposes it is as if he is actually living it. Then, as the plane plummets into the sea he 'saves' his double only to recognize and be re-identified with him in death. Again in 'Blow-Up', the narrator becomes so involved in a photograph he has taken and with 'saving' a young man in it that he loses his mind and any firm sense of the grammatical first person. In 'Lejana' a woman discovers her double emerging out of the mist, from the other side of a bridge.[1]

The plank-scene is Cortázar's subtlest and most dramatic exploration of the limits of identity. In the first place neither of the two characters involved is 'fixed' in relation to the other; or, more accurately, the terms of their correspondence are continually switched. Oliveira is 'really' the traveller; yet though Traveler has always stayed at home in Buenos Aires he thinks of himself as a 'failed nomad'. And Oliveira is by no means confirmed in the role of traveller; when he is in Buenos Aires he may feel Paris is his home, but the opposite is also true, just as paradoxically. By turns their identity or identities are explicitly referred to the 'zones' they inhabit. For example, the suspicion that Talita may never arrive with the promised *maté* (the base of Argentina's national drink), together with the fact that Gekrepten badly wants to make him some coffee, provokes Oliveira into momentarily dividing the street into sides dedicated respectively to those beverages. Alternatively Oliveira claims he inhabits the polar region, in improbable but convincing contrast to the tropics which evidently envelop Traveler, and Talita when she sets out on her sweaty journey across the plank. The dialogue between the two is sustained by such inventive attempts at location with their ever superimposed ironies (who is finally more the gaucho, more the

Argentinian? and so on). For Oliveira at least, the exchange is part of an unsubstitutable game, in which his existence is at stake. It constitutes his most radical and brilliant attempt to 'jump over the line', to get out of his square (*casilla*) and 'those things you can't do anything about', in the hopscotch route from earth to heaven, Igdrassil.

When Talita is closest to him, within half a yard or so, he leans forward and stretches out his hand. In the final and potentially most pathetic twist, he, the voyager of zones (Apollinaire gives an important epigraph to the novel), is left behind, his hand outstretched for the farther shore, *amore*, like the lonely unburied souls who wander for one hundred years by the Styx in the *Aeneid*. Cortázar lets only a hint of the pathos through, however, focusing next, without more ado and as if wilfully, on the progress of Talita's bum returning backwards inch by inch across the plank to home on the other side.

In *Hopscotch*, Cortázar contrives with conspicuous success to say serious things about a condition deeply familiar to him, as a self-confessed 'argentino afrancesado' (a Frenchified Argentine), without lapsing into solemnity or portentousness. His earlier works tell this truth less well, and tend to be therapeutic and cathartic rather than metaphysical, as he himself has said. He began his career as a lyric poet (under the pseudonym Julio Denis) and has repeatedly confirmed that that stance is no good for him, up to his recent collection *Pameos y meopas* (1971),[2] where he reduces a universe reminiscent of Oliveira's with one fell swoop to the tawdriest of foundations ('1950, Año del Libertador', for example, simplistically mocks the fate of the middle-class Argentinian whose every outlet is frustrated and who pays in quarterly instalments for land once grandly taken, by the Libertador San Martín, during the war of Independence). In his second book *The Kings* (*Los reyes*, 1949), a long dialogue with the Minotaur, he modified the Mallarméan detachment of his first poems. But it was only in his first novel *The Winners* (*Los premios*, 1960) that he made a significant advance on all this, and on the self-enclosing perfection of his early short-stories. In *The Winners* a set of eminently Argentine characters is described on a cruise towards unknown destinations, their prize in a national competition. The social and moral forces they 'represent' in themselves and in their intercourse positively invite decipherment, and some critics have been content simply to outline what they see as the author's allegorical or satirical tactics. In practice this has meant reading the novel despite itself, and despite the 'central' character Persio, an autonomous intelligence who nevertheless remains a 'fellow-passenger'. *The Winners* is much more importantly an exploration of the novel as a form, a narrative endeavouring to make virtue out of the necessary arbitrariness of its patternings. However, it is marred by digressiveness within a monotonously constant situation (the petrified kingdom of Polydectes in the myth of Perseus), and by the hint of intellectual pretension given by the name Perseus itself.

How Cortázar moved from here even while writing *Hopscotch* is shown in his decision to abandon the 'heavy' title he had originally thought to give this novel: *Mandala*. At this period he generally came to display a new attitude of radical irreverence towards literary forms and conventions, first announced in the uneven *Cronopios and Famas* (*Historias de cronopios y famas*, 1962). Here Cortázar presents us with sketches for stories, over-candid personal confessions, possible geographies and extravagant situations, fit for his whimsical characters, the cautious Famas and the prodigal Cronopios. Furthermore, literary practice is demonstrated before the reader, out of a kit as it were (one of the sections is called 'Instruction Manual'). This process is taken even further in *Hopscotch*, which while retaining the appearance of a novel can be put together by the reader in at least two ways.[3] The whole is prefaced by instructions on how to read it, either from chapter one to chapter fifty-six (in which case chapters, or entries, 57–155 become dispensable), or in a sequence beginning 73–1–2–116–3. . . The integrity of the narrative is further broken down by occasional use of the device of telling two entirely separate stories on alternate lines, a concentration of the effect perceptible in Gekrepten and Talita's totally divorced conversations with Oliveira in the plank scene. Spanish prose itself, like the prose of Joyce's *Ulysses*, is assigned to a range of conscious styles, not least in Oliveira's own word-games and other literary experiments, and in his bizarre and often hilarious phonetics (the 'reasonable' substitution of 'c' and 'qu' with 'k', and the ironically pompous addition of the silent 'h', as in 'Horacio Holiveira'). Cortázar undermines literary language out of sympathy with Oliveira's irreverence.

For, despite the instability of his literary surroundings and the uninsured course of the narrative, Oliveira remains the one who holds the novel together as such in any of its readings. As a character he has been criticized as improbable and contrived, far too intellectual for the 'average *porteño*' he claims to be in the text. His soliloquies and contributions to debates, especially during his early Paris days and nights, have been objected to as showy and essentially un-novelesque, more appropriate indeed to the windy Dr Morelli, who philosophizes at length in some of the dispensable chapters of the book. Average *porteño* Oliveira may well not be; but if it is true that his case against western modes of apprehension and dialectics is made better in his antics than in his philosophizing,[4] then he performs more than enough of these for the case to be made. For example, his groping for an errant sugar lump under the tables of a restaurant in chapter one works well as an exploration of fixation and chance which never exceeds its enacted humour; the scene further anticipates Oliveira's supreme performance jousting with Traveler for Talita.

Yet, ingenious as he is, Oliveira is by no means always allowed to be up front, Cortázar's showpiece spokesman. As the performer of antics and verbal pataphysician he is given many breaks, it is true: his seesaw-questions; the verbal flights he wins from the Cemetery (the Dictionary of the Spanish Royal Academy); his savage parodies of the nineteenth-century Spanish realist Pérez Galdós, or of *Reader's Digest*; his comments on Cambaceres's heroes and Martínez Estrada's essays on Argentina; and his own written compositions like the 'Typical Dialogue between Spaniards' are all presented unapologetically, without authorial intervention. But elsewhere the reader feels a hint of distancing. Talita communicates directly, cutting him out; or he is fobbed off in a generalization, about professional suicides for example, which exposes Cortázar's reservations towards him.

Cortázar's whole implicit relationship with Oliveira, the uncompromising and dedicated player, can in fact usefully be compared with that between the characters in 'The Pursuer' ('El perseguidor'),[5] a short story which Cortázar has linked with *Hopscotch* on this and other counts. There he embarked on the awesome task of describing the soul of a 'great' artist, the saxo-phonist Johnny Carter (inspired by Charlie Parker, to whom 'The Pursuer' is dedicated), with no more than the thin first person of Bruno, Johnny's biographer, as his formal medium. At first the message is easy to get, deceptively so as in *The Winners*: Carter is an angelic brute, the sax-sex, all feeling, incapable of understanding his own musical creation or its larger import; Bruno is the self-effacing, committed helper whose highest ambi-tion is to communicate Johnny's art to others through his reviews and his biography. This pattern is soon upset however by Bruno's disquieting discovery that he doesn't know when Johnny is serious, when he the critic is being fooled by this 'cunning chim-panzee' who turns out to know Dylan Thomas's poems. Further involvement with Johnny in his jazz milieu makes him unpleas-antly conscious of being superfluous, parasitic and empty. This leads to an ironically obvious self-assertion in Bruno's record: Johnny is a promiscuous animal, a junkie whose freaky reality is artificially stimulated, and so on. At the same time he presses his own prestige as a writer to absurd extremes: Johnny becomes so much the stuffed trophy of his pursuit, so much set in his Negro background and in musical history, that by continuing to live he can only be a potential threat to the ideas Bruno has sold to his public.

'The Pursuer' is a very intense and quite nasty story, in which people lose badly, and Bruno ends up as the profaner of the very communication he had claimed to be devoting his life to achiev-ing. To this extent Johnny Carter is right to call Bruno's language 'filthy', and to hint at the necessary obscenity of all writing 'about' art. Yet he cannot express his own, or 'jump over the line', except with his instrument; he cannot otherwise handle himself and crumbles when the music stops.

In Oliveira, Cortázar discovered or invented a less terrifying partner, or *alter ego*: one he could work with in better faith, further from the apocalyptic edge. Oliveira presents none of the problems of 'genius' and has no instrument beyond his words and actions. But he is a wholly dedicated player and bears many similarities to Johnny. In Paris he feels himself to be American, the victim of culture mongers; he is pursued by parasitic incom-prehension; he is also the adoptive father of a dead child whose memory haunts him as Bee's haunts Johnny. At his height Oliveira is an artist-in-a-novel testing the limits of the form, in an alliance with his biographer denied altogether to the litterateur Bruno and the saxophonist who (in a final twist) bears Cortázar's own initials in his name. So that despite occasional pricks from Cortázar and despite an eventual fate perhaps as ignominious as Johnny Carter's, Oliveira is entrusted as plenipotentiary with the dominant scenes in the book. He may simply be the one who shows up contorted values in another 'artist', as the genial escort of Berthe Trépat for example. After her bizarre performance at the piano in a near-empty hall, he takes her home in the rain soothing her paranoia, a wiser artist through whom the insights and the humour come:

> 'Beauty, exaltation, the golden bough,' said Berthe Trépat. 'Don't say anything, I can guess it perfectly. I too came to Paris from Pau, some years ago now, looking for the golden bough. But I have been weak, young, I've been. . .But what's your name?'
> 'Oliveira,' said Oliveira.
> 'Oliveira. . .*Des olives*, the Mediterranean. . .I too am from the South, we're panic, young man, we're panic the two of us. Not like Valentin, who's from Lille. . .'

More ambitiously, Oliveira may pretend to enter heaven, the 'kibbutz of desire', the great 'Obscure', and see 'the true figure of the world, *patterns pretty as can be*', in the revelation of art and game. These particular words come to him as he is being carted away by the Paris police, along with the ageing prostitute Emmanuele and two fags, in an atmosphere of orgasmic degradation heavily reminiscent of Johnny Carter's world.

It is through Oliveira that Cortázar gauges the kind of Latin American artist he is more finely than most of his contemporaries have done for themselves, and less crudely than elsewhere in his own work. Besides the crucial and painful re-encounter with 'home-truth' in the form of Traveler across the plank there are other evaluative moments of dramatic brilliance in the novel. In chapter 13 for example, Ronald, Babs, and other members of the 'Club' (as they call it) which Oliveira belongs to in Paris, are lying around listening to some old seventy-eights. During one number Babs is swaying on Ronald's knees since 'the theme was vulgar enough for her to take liberties which Ronald would never condone when Satchmo sang *Yellow Dog Blues*'. Raised to an Olympian viewpoint by a mixture of music, sauerkraut and vodka, she condescends to look down at Oliveira with his eskimo skin, 'smoking and now hopelessly drunk, with a resentful, bitter South-American face whose mouth would smile from time to time between drags, Oliveira's lips which Babs had once desired (not now) were curved a little while the rest of the face looked washed-out and absent. However much he liked jazz Oliveira would never join in the game like Ronald, for him it'd be good or bad, hot or cool, white or black, traditional or modern, Chicago or New Orleans, never jazz, never this thing which Satchmo, Ronald and Babs now were'. And so on, about Armstrong, in the kind of language Bruno used, finally putting Armstrong down too. Oliveira then bravely remarks how wild a success Armstrong is at the moment in Buenos Aires, admitting that his country is pure *réchauffé*. 'Starting with you,' says someone else. 'You've come here following the pattern of all your compatriots who go off to Paris to get their 'sentimental education'. Oliveira admits he may be right: 'Where I should really be is playing pool with Traveler. You don't know him, do you. You don't know a thing about all that. So what's the use of talking about it?'

In this case, in Paris, the 'other side', Oliveira's retreat into silence is aggressive, into presumed strength. After all, Babs does appear faintly ridiculous on her pedestal, with her cultural snob-bishness, accusing the poor South American Oliveira of being un-able to do more than 'read the labels', of being irremediably precluded as a full participant in the games of her 'Club'. But the trouble is, his domestic 'side', his obscure games of pool with Traveler, simply don't interest his sentimental educators. Games may be universal but players aren't. So that when back in Buenos Aires he accuses Traveler of the very limitations Babs had attribu-ted to him he is no better off.

The ceremonial encounter with Traveler over the plank in fact marks a turning point. From then on he slips; his unfortunate grab at Talita in the cold-room is followed by guilt and uncer-tainty. He gives ground, imagining pursuit, and finally barricades himself in his room. He is discovered there, in his last retreat (the theme incidentally of the short story 'House Taken Over', 'Casa tomada'), saying to himself, as he sits by the open window:

> in the end there must be some encounter, although it couldn't last longer than that terribly sweet instant in which the best thing would without doubt have been to lean just a little bit out and let oneself go, splat it's over.

The splat could be the end of his reason or of his life, or both (Cortázar himself claims not to know which): the concentrated expiation of impossible ambition and 'unreasonable' demand, the last move towards Igdrassil in the hopscotch game.

Cortázar makes his character lose a game no-one could be expected to win, caught as he is in the paradox of the two epigraphs of the novel (Vaché: 'Rien ne vous tue un homme comme d'être obligé de representer un pays'; Apollinaire: 'Il faut voyager loin en aimant sa maison'), and of his general epistemology. But in so far as it is through him that the novel is carried as a venture, his awareness of the odds becomes a statement of his author's artistic morality:

> Lay quietism, moderate ataraxy, attentive inattention. The important thing for Oliveira was to witness, unfainting, the spectacle of this Tupac-Amaru dismemberment, not to relapse into the poor egocentricity. . .which was daily proclaimed around him in every possible form.

This 'lay quietism' differs importantly from the prostrate quietism of the heroes of Borges's *Fictions,* who are clear that all novelesque exploration of reality in this 'setting part of time' is pointless from the start. For Tupac Amaru (the Quechua rebel leader who was killed by the Spanish in 1781) is important not just anatomically but as an American in Oliveira's and Cortázar's divisive reality. In other words a recognizable geography can be perceived in the abstract patterns of *Hopscotch*, with its journeys in simultaneity, its rapid ironies and the spiralling humour of Horacio Oliveira, *heimatlos*, artist portrayed.

By any standards *Hopscotch* eclipses all Cortázar had written before it; the novel also stands as a point of reference for what has come afterwards. *62* (1968), for example, takes its very title from chapter 62 of *Hopscotch*, where we duly discover some notes on a book planned by Cortázar's scholarly alias Dr Morelli. This book would dispense with 'old fashioned' ideas of individual psychology and character, and explore in art the implications of modern neurobiology, in a plot suggestive of man's eventual capacity to transcend himself after all, something which *62*, as an 'assemble-it-yourself' or model kit (*modelo para armar*), does with less than total ingenuousness. Morelli appears again[6] in *Round the Day in Eighty Worlds* (*La vuelta al día en ochenta mundos*, 1967) amid camp illustrations and ornate echoes of Jules Verne. But a more intimate and important connection may be found with *Manuel's Book* (*Libro de Manuel*, 1973), which may properly be considered the sequel to *Hopscotch*.

The parallels between the Parisian part of *Hopscotch* and *Manuel's Book* couldn't be missed by anybody. The 'Club' of expatriates in the French capital, with their distinctive cultural enthusiasms (Fritz Lang, Hindu philosophy, and so on), reappears as the less decorously named group 'The Joda'. As the male pair between whom the author locates himself, Oliveira and Traveler are replaced by Marcos and Andrés, the female duo La Maga–Talita being played now by Ludmilla–Francine. We even have a replay of the 'boy-child' undertone, Rocamadour surviving longer now as the (Im)manuel for whom indeed the book within the book is created, as we shall see. It is as if Cortázar himself was determined that the two novels shouldn't fail to be compared, so that the differences between them could be better gauged.

We enter *Manuel's Book* to discover that the party is over; someone has definitely fallen out of the window. The change of mood is most obvious in the political awareness of The Joda as a predominantly Latin American group, and in the way this awareness is related (via Sade and Rousseau) to man's nature as a sexual creature. As far as amorous practice goes, even to points of detail, the difference between the two books might be compared with that which, over the same decade, separates, say, *Irma la Douce* from *Last Tango in Paris*. Throughout the novel we are held close to the political realities of Latin America, and the West as a whole, by means of newspaper and other clippings, typographically untranslated and set into the text as they are selected and discussed by the characters engaged in compiling a scrapbook-testament for the use of baby Manuel in maturer years. As a constant in the narrative (in part the product of Cortázar's work as a translator for UNESCO)[7] we find reports of gratuitous police attacks on students and professors in France; guerrilla attacks on foreign embassies in Uruguay (FARO, Tupamaros) and Brazil; a demonstration in Heidelberg against the presence of the U.S. Secretary of State for Defence, Robert McNamara; political trials and imprisonings in the Soviet Union; violations of human rights reported by Amnesty International; police torture in Brazil (which reminds the character Heredia of how his own arm was broken three times during interrogation in São Paulo); military aid given to Latin American states via the U.S. organization Southcom; and so on. The narrative itself concentrates on how the main characters effectively absorb this distressing information into their 'private' lives and matches extremities of political with sexual behaviour, as if in an ultimate attempt to believe that man is not vile. The historical urgency increases steadily towards the extensive and devastating quotations from Mark Lane's *Conversations with North Americans* near the close of the novel.

What had been a hint or nuance in *Hopscotch* is now made explicit and located. The Latin Americans of The Joda, emigrés who are given no 'this side' to return to, are by the same token not allowed to elude their origins as easily as Oliveira had done, nor the responsibilities they entail. For example, in their restaging of it, the imaginary figures of Oliveira's 'Typical Dialogue between Spaniards' turn out to be definitely reactionary. And as a 'cultural area' ever suspicious of the 'free jazz' within itself, the U.S. now actively menaces or controls Latin American states which appear far less remote than Oliveira's homeland, seen from Paris, thanks to the personal letters and other means of communication which supplement the ground-bass of the press-clippings. Even the doodlings of the characters in this book locate the *terra incognita* of Latin America in time and space. And imagining the conversation between certain U.S.-trained Latin American counterrevolutionaries eating at Fouquet's ('in Paris, capital of France and cradle of the revolution inspired, it had to be acknowledged, by that of the United States who had trained these commandos so efficiently to fight against the revolutionaries of Latin America'),

Cortázar chooses to make them talk *porteño*, adding, not altogether playfully, that just some of the linguistic alternatives for imaginary 'Latin American' conversations included:

ibero-
lusitano-
italico
maya-quiché   etc } americano 1970
yoruba
uralo-altaico
incasico

This does not mean that Cortázar loses any of his brilliance. Some of the more trivial press cuttings (local boxing news from Chile; an astrological advertisement) serve as a hilarious counterweight; and the commentaries made on the selected 'evidence' generally by the group, as a mediator between the public and the private, are genial and humorous. Here are Susana and the group translating a reader's letter from Etienne Metreau, a 20-year-old in Grenoble, gratuitously assaulted by the police:

> On the afternoon of Saturday 6th, as I was walking in the campus at Saint-Martin-d'Hères to watch the students and learn the reason for their violence,
> Here allow me a smile, since this business of still not understanding the reason for their violence almost justifies what happened to poor Etienne,
> I was invited to attend the 'boom-barricade'. That evening I approached the avenue along the campus. A car stopped in front of me. A squad of seven men gets out.
> This change of tense is a little harsh in Spanish.
> 'Forget the commentary, dear,' said Patricio.

Even the 'heaviest' information is leavened by wit, for example in the half-echoes between Andrés and Francine's love-making and Heredia's subsequent urbane account of how to seduce English girls. Similar internal balances are struck between a scene in a decadent Paris night club and a cheery Prensa Latina telex about a non-day in Castro's Cuba, with which it is subtly juxtaposed.

Nevertheless we must see Cortázar's inquisition into his own and others' political integrity as the deliberate and profaning gesture which he announces it to be at the beginning of the book:

> There is no doubt that the things which happen here couldn't happen in such an unlikely fashion, while the pure elements of imagination find themselves derogated by frequent remissions to the everyday and the concrete. Personally I don't regret this heterogeneity which luckily no longer seems to be that to me after a long process of convergence; if for years I have written texts dealing with the problems of Latin America, at the same time as novels and stories in which these problems were absent or appeared only tangentially, here and now the currents have merged, though reconciling them hasn't been at all easy, as is perhaps evident from the confused and tormented itinerary of one or other character.

The situation is no longer appropriate to preferential focusing on the irresolution of Oliveira, and still less on the 'instinctive' artistry of Johnny, existentially sacred as they may be. The best of it all, of course, not at all out of keeping with his own keen sense of dilemma, is that Cortázar should have touched the political agony of Latin America so surely, having himself moved over to the 'other side' to become a French citizen.

JOSÉ MARÍA ARGUEDAS

She always had that hair in her damp mouth. It crossed one side of her face, and all the skies contrasted in that arc which made saliva rise at one corner of her lips. The towering, constricted clouds, the small movement of the qopayso, mountain grass, wavered in that arc; and more so when Fidela began to cry. I was behind doña Fabiana, hanging on her shawl. Again the traveller, that unknown woman, looked at me meaningfully, and knelt before the cook, kissed the edge of her skirt. Then she began to go up the great ridge, all rugged and bleak. We watched her go for a long time. She passed behind the thorns which served as a pen for a colt belonging to the lady of the village, and began to go up the scree slope. 'So she's going to give birth to an orphan, a stranger; somewhere,' said doña Fabiana. She had already gone up very high; she couldn't come back.

THE FOX FROM ABOVE: *Fidela pregnant; blood; she went. The boy was confused. He also was a stranger. He went down to your territory.*

THE FOX FROM BELOW: *An unknown sex confuses boys like him. Whores swear and whore rightly. They distanced the said boy still further. The whore's 'vixen' belongs to no-one; it's of the world down here, of my territory. Flower of mire, they say of them. In their 'vixens' fear appears and sureness too.*

THE FOX FROM ABOVE: *Sureness, fear too, estrangedness are born of the Virgin and the* ima sapra; *and of iron twisted, twisted again, stopped in movement, because it wants to order the exit and entry of everything.*

THE FOX FROM BELOW: *Hee, hee, hee. . .! Down here the sugar cane flowers are panaches which dance tickling the cloth that swaddles the heart of those who are able to speak; cotton is white* ima sapra. *But the serpent* amaru *will not end. Iron throws out smoke, blood, makes the brain burn, the testicle too.*

THE FOX FROM ABOVE: *So it is. Let's go on looking and learning. . .*

1. Chaucato set sail in his smack 'Sampson I', taking his ten fishermen as a crew, among them the fairy Dumb, and as an extra, on trial, a violinist from the fancy night-club 'The Black Cat'.

El zorro de arriba y el zorro de abajo (Buenos Aires, 1971). *The Fox from Above and the Fox from Below.* End of the First Diary and start of chapter 1.

The two foxes talking are the titular guardians of Arguedas's last book, only parts of which were published before his death. They emerge suddenly at the end of the long diary, written in an Andean village in 1968, which introduces the book: a precarious record of his state of mind, of his faltering attempts to write his novel and get Chaucato under way down in Chimbote in the world below, and of his origins as the 'confused' boy whom the foxes chuckle over having watched Fidela disappear into the mountains. From this diary we learn that Arguedas, on psychiatric advice, is writing as a way of fending off death, of postponing a suicide attempt more successful than the one which 'maimed' him in 1944.[1] From the outset, then, the work is infused with the pressure he feels at his own neck; this is kept up by subsequent diary entries made in Chile and Peru the following year and introduced later on into the novel proper. The means and the moment of suicide are chosen at last, and the narrative of the second part was left hanging in the air, authorless, like the foxes themselves, after Arguedas shot himself on 29 November 1969. The book's power, however, goes far beyond that of a personal testimony from the edge between life and death.

As a posthumous work, *The Fox from Above and the Fox from Below* is an odd arrangement of diary and narrative proper. Part I, the bulk of the book, includes a First Diary (May 1968), two chapters of the novel, a Second Diary (February–March 1969), two further chapters and a Third Diary (May 1969), Part II is simply a last diary (August–October 1969) and the Epilogue is a letter consigning the unfinished manuscript to the publishers. Under the apparent artlessness of this arrangement and of Arguedas's prose lies a large and firm purpose, at moments brilliantly realized. Arguedas, *in extremis*, achieves broad coherences as he moves via the foxes, at the end of the First Diary, from 'open' confession to straight impersonal narrative. In the Diaries he uses the existential anguish of 'to be or not to be' as a convention by which to locate himself more accurately in his circumstances. He says who he 'is' by inference, by measuring himself, for example, against people nominally most like him, that is, other Latin American novelists. His extreme situation allows him to be free and outspoken. Professing impatience with professionality he speaks with especial warmth of writers like Juan Rulfo, and the Brazilian Guimarães Rosa, in touch like him with the heart of a hidden, abandoned America, which he calls provincial with witting provocation. He admires García Márquez also, if only for his insight into its secular isolation; and Onetti, 'who trembles in every word'. Ranged on the other side he sees Fuentes, clever and insubstantial; Cortázar who was publicly provoked by this attack[2] (as we learn from the Third Diary) to lament the sentimentality of the provincial writer; and Carpentier, a 'famous European' who happens to speak Spanish.

Clearly Arguedas's weapons are not those normally acceptable, thus exposed, in literary criticism. And it is true that rather than the dry strength of the dialogues in *Pedro Páramo* he will evoke Rulfo's emotional centre as a man, and deliberately confuse him with the half-Indian mentor of his own childhood, Felipe Maywa, a worker employed by his step-mother in the mountains. Also that his friend Mario Vargas Llosa, whom he recognizes as his literary champion,[3] emerges not as the magisterial orchestrator of novels very different from his own but as one who fully understood him for what he has been. As he says in the Third Diary, Arguedas saw himself as someone

who played in his childhood making wavy and sometimes
straight chains of nits dug from his head, and cracked them
then with his nails, really pleased with the noise they made
. . .who began his formal education in a language [Spanish]
he didn't love and which all but infuriated him, at the age of
fourteen, when most children have finished or nearly finished
theirs. . .Why should it not be true that this individual
should have had difficulties understanding Joyce's *Ulysses*
and should still have them trying to follow Lezama Lima, so
densely and unscrupulously urban? That he should have
abandoned, upset and somewhat horrified – at the age of 21
– the reading of *Les Chants de Maldoror* and should
nevertheless have drunk like sustaining, almost intimate
aqua regia *Une Saison dans l'enfer, Leaves of Grass, Trilce,*
the tragedies of Shakespeare and Sophocles? Isn't this a
respectable, truly Indo-Hispanic reaction? Mario understood
it to be so, and for that reason instead of discounting the
results of that experience appreciates them enthusiastically.
And I understand at the same time why Cortázar, over-
sensitive and perhaps half-faint with the stench of the
streets, should be brought even to anger by my confession.

From here, still a guileless series of diary entries, Arguedas goes
on to elaborate what he means by provincial. He describes a
small fiesta, a performance of 'typical' Chilean folk dances, which
a friend had taken him to. The extreme commercialization of it
all causes him to think by contrast of the 'de-vilified' man of Cuba
and of the fiestas of the Peruvian highlands. He then imagines the
probable reactions to these fiestas, 'untouched by vanity and
lucre', of the writers he has mentioned. Rulfo and García Márquez
who would understand them from within, and Fuentes, who
wouldn't, and Carpentier, who considering 'our indigenous things'
merely as excellent material, would draw erudite analogies with
'the Greeks, Assyrians, Javanese and a hundred other names, rare
and correct'. Being his kind of provincial writer in Latin America
is thus subtly made a matter of ideological commitment. Continuing to reside in her cities or in Europe means involvement with
a destructive (capitalist) system which few can withstand (a
thought which echoes Rousseau, of course, and, more immediately,

Régis Debray or Che Guevara's theories of guerrilla-led revolution).

Arguedas further escapes the charge of simple self-indulgence and hidden resentment by the great delicacy and lack of animus with which he expresses himself. In this way he is able to expose so much more of his formation, in the full sense of the word, that greater values are necessarily seen to be implicated in his 'case'. As a leitmotif in the First Diary there hovers the *huayronqo*, an insect a cross between hummingbird and fly, intensely black, which flies with its legs dangling down, to land helplessly on the plush face of a flower, inebriated to the point of paralysis. In so far as the spirit of this creature, peculiar to the Andes, pervades these pages, Arguedas incidentally realizes that ambition to name American creatures better than Carpentier ever did. The *huayronqo* hovers to more purpose as the unmistakable omen of death in the Quechua-speaking world Arguedas grew up in, and as a self-incarnation whose separate identity is nevertheless wholly respected: 'The pressure I feel in the whole of my head because of the poison must bear a certain relationship with the flight of the *huayronqo*, stained with cemeterial pollen'.

The 'poison' itself, the source of addiction, is then revealed at last, with electric finesse, in the last entry of the opening diary. Fidela, a *mestiza*, arrives, from Ukuhuay where the heavy ivy-like *ima sapra* grow, pale-grey, entwining their roots in the bark of trees which over-hang the precipices there. She is travelling alone, herself heavy in pregnancy, and penniless. Arguedas's account of their tenderness as they lay together in the yard, how she lifted and held him over her, and their 'sweet denigrated secret', is both controlled and agonized as a moment of encounter never surpassed. This is the start of the enduring 'confusion' referred to by the foxes after Fidela goes away for good the next morning. The 'symbols' and allusions of these opening pages, the *huayronqo*, the *ima sapra*, Arguedas's own 'twisted iron' and the serpent *amaru*, could be professionally reduced in some Freudian or other account of them. But the prose runs persistently counter to such 'explanation', and conveys knowledge with its own 'circles and depths', and palpably flows in phrase and paragraph from another culture, that of the foxes whom he makes guardians of this, his last book.

To have pressed deeper into intimacy, to have dragged out the last ounce of confession, would clearly have been hazardous at this point. And as if in order to keep writing, Arguedas switches abruptly from himself as centre to the third persons of the foxes. These two 'characters', who give the novel its title, are taken from an important Quechua narrative collected by Francisco de Avila in the sixteenth century and translated by Arguedas in 1966 under the Spanish title *Dioses y hombres de Huarochirí*.[4] They appear in chapter 5 of this work, when Huatyacuri, a hero from the early epic stages of Quechua history, has fallen asleep. He has just travelled from the sea coast up to the highlands or Andes, where, we are told, there lives a man named Tamtañamca, rich, attractive to his fellows and apparently wise, but afflicted by a mysterious disease. From the conversation of the two foxes, the one from 'Above' (the Andes) and the other from 'Below' (the coast), Huatyacuri learns the secret cause of Tamtañamca's diease: a poisonous creature in the roof of his house and a double-headed toad under his wife's millstone denote her infidelity but also, and here more to the point, his failing creativity. Huatyacuri then finds the means of curing Tamtañamca, but not without admonishing him in the lapidary phrase: 'If you were really creative you could not be ill'.

In Arguedas's book the language of the foxes is difficult and elliptical. But their authority to judge him, a modern Tamtañamca, and their serene humour are clear. The difficulty of their words in Arguedas's prose – they sound as strange in Spanish as they do in English – comes from the depth to which they are steeped in Quechua thought. Indeed, they later break out in this language at length, leaving Arguedas, as it were, to provide a translation. For example, the 'unknown sex' mentioned by the Fox from Below, may mean a woman's sex; but it also means sex beyond the rigid gender-division of European languages, as the complement of 'creativity'. The 'twisted iron' referred to by the Fox from Above, and the snake *amaru*, are consequently not just phallic; *amaru* is more properly the life-body of the mountain rivers, of Indian and of his own survival.

Like Asturias, Arguedas got to know the Indians of his country when still a child. After his mother's death (when he was only three) and his father's second marriage to a rich landowner, he spent most of his time in their company, in the mountain areas of Peru, near Andahuaylas and Puquio. Unlike Asturias, he learnt their language, and became more proficient in it than in Spanish. As he himself tells us, his formal education in Spanish began only in 1924; and on the death of his father in 1931 he went to the University of San Marcos in Lima. There he came under the influence of the Marxist José Carlos Mariátegui, and of the young Apristas (then a socialist party), and began to publish: his novella *Agua* (1935) was strongly autobiographical, like much of his writing; and a brief imprisonment in 1937 was later reflected in the novel *El sexto* (1961). More important, he announced what the Quechua language and perception meant to him in *Canto Kechwa* (1938, translated into English under the bizarre title *The Singing Mountaineers*, Austin 1957). There, as in a number of subsequent works, supported in part by academic and anthropological institutions, he showed himself less interested in evoking the glorious and ancient civilization of the Andes than in the survival of a way of life in which he had come to feel himself deeply implicated (from speaking Quechua as a child he went on to write and publish in it as a living, though little read language).[5] To try and deny Pizarro and the Spanish conquest, to reject everything that the Spaniards brought to America and to indulge a notion of lost purity, seemed to him absurd and (in its way) an escape. Other Andean writers preceded him in this sentiment, saliently the Marxist Mariátegui[6] who stressed the Indian and *mestizo* (mixed-blood) element in Peruvian reality. Arguedas succeeded in incorporating it into literature, being particularly sensitive to the language, the music and the written texts of the Quechua. Other novels in the Andean 'Indianist' tradition, by Alcides Arguedas, Jorge Icaza or the celebrated Ciro Alegría,[7] lack the kind of credible centre substantiated by Arguedas in his novels and poems, and in his presentation of Quechua folk songs and stories, and post-Hispanic myths about dead heroes like Tupac Amaru, or the headless 'Inkarrey'[8] waiting to return to life and entirety.

In the first of his novels, *Yawar fiesta* (1941; revised in 1958), the break between the worlds of the two foxes, the Indian sierra and the Spanish coast is, however not purely linguistic. Andean traditions threatened by national policies emanating from the coast are passionately defended not just by Indians but by the white señores who have come to live with them. Both groups find a common emblem in the fiesta of blood, or bulls, indicated in the title, which despite its Iberian origin has become so much part of the mountain environment that for either group to lose it would be to lose part of themselves. This is an early work with more than a hint of the folkloric in it, of fond childhood memory: and although Quechua songs reverberate in his prose their presence is far from indispensable. Emphasis shifted strongly in his next major novel, *The Deep Rivers* (*Los ríos profundos*, 1958).[9] Here resistance is made both more comprehensive as such and more dependent on indigenous language and myth. The moment of actual physical conflict between Indians and their enemies – their march into Abancay – is significantly not shared or even witnessed by Ernesto, a transparent persona of the author. But it still remains open to him to resolve painful knowledge of duality in himself into certain symbols and emblems of traditional Peru. The most prominent of these is the *zumbayllu*, the etymologically hybrid humming top (Spanish *zumbar* and Quechua *yllu*) which pierces the imagination of Ernesto and his companions, 'awakening memories of the deep rivers themselves' and expressing with its ending '*yllu*' a whole shimmering cycle in Quechua thought which also involves phenomena like the vibrant *pinkuyllu* (an arched flute) and the buzzing, honey-tailed *tankayllu*. Moreover, natural emblems like these exist in the novel as they do in Quechua, not as pathetic fallacy (Wordsworth: 'I saw them feel or linked them to some feeling' – the alternatives being much the same), but with that otherness and independence which Levi-Strauss and the structuralists have detected in 'savage' thought and which constitutes Arguedas's main point.

In *Every Blood* (*Todas las sangres*, 1964) conflict develops into sustained rebellion. The Indians take over land and begin to resettle it, remembering the *ayllu* or communal agricultural system of their ancestors. Helped by the articulate example of the main character Rendon Willka, exploited miners and *colonos* see a way of becoming modern *comuneros*. Their new life is brutally destroyed by the police, as Ilóm's Maya were by white poison. But their act, the child of myth, transforms that myth into a possible revolutionary programme: the vindication of the *ayllu*

and the communal agricultural practices which have lived on in
the Andes since pre-Columbian times. The way of life which had
earned the Incas their reputation as socialists among the Enlightenment thinkers of Europe would thus be restored to their descendants as a viable modern economy.[10] Because of this, Willka
resembles not so much an isolated, fragmented and finally 'alien'
hero, like Ilóm, as the great figure of his own Andean past, Tupac
Amaru, who had led the massive rising against the Spanish in 1781,
and whom Arguedas had celebrated two years before *Every
Blood* in a hymn written in Quechua (*Tupac Amaru Kamaq
Taytanchisman. Haylli-Taki*, 1962). His prose in the novel (which
some critics have wanted to call an epic) is decidedly unpatroniz-
ing and unfolkloric. It marks the high point of his confidence in
the socialist revolution and of his capacity to understand it in
Indian terms.[11] The life of Rendon and his people becomes pro-
gressively re-saturated with the Quechua songs which Arguedas
has known in oral tradition, and dominant among these are their
collective work songs, the *wankas*. The immense poetry of these
pieces sustains Rendon and his band under the fire of hired
soldiers, who themselves cannot remain wholly insensitive:

> The guard from Ayacucho who had looked during the
> whole descent for the *comunero* who ran away, to kill him,
> and the sergeant himself stood still for a good while. This
> collaboration and the song brought back their childhood.
> A deep star began to beat in the blood of both of them, like
> the sun rising over the calm or wind-stirred lakes of the
> highland:

Wayanaysi rapran	The swallow moves its wings
manaya k'an hinachu,	not so much as you,
mak'ta, runa	boy, man.
K'ollk'e chalway ahujan	The silver-needle fish moves
	through water
mayu k'ochapi,	in river and lake
manaya k'an hinachu	not so much as you,
mak'ta, runa	boy, man.

As a further event in this series of novels, *The Fox from Above
and the Fox from Below* is richer, and unresolved to the point of

torture. The four chapters of the novel itself, intercalated between the diary entries and dialogues, contain the most violent of his internal tensions and contradictions, but do not themselves generate the end Arguedas put to it. The book as a whole is thus a special testament of failure of an earlier vision. Despite his supreme effort, Arguedas's last redoubts of hope were threatened by changes round him more rapid than any he could make in himself, and of which he refused to be merely the spectator. In the Second Diary he writes: 'In *Every Blood*, the Andean *yawar mayu* (river of blood) conquers, and conquers well. That is my own victory. But now I can't start on chapter 3 of this new novel, because it inflames me though I don't fully understand what is happening in Chimbote and in the world.'

All the Indians in this last novel have come down in an avalanche (*lloqlla*) from their traditional home in the mountains to the coast, not even to the slums of Lima (that was an 'old' problem) but to Chimbote, a boom fishing-town to the north where degradation and oppression reach extremes that are hallucinatory despite Arguedas's habitual realist control of his prose. This wholesale loss of a culture in a South-American cannery row owned by Japanese capital seemed to Arguedas symptomatic of Peru as he saw it towards the end of his life. In the four chapters of the novel Asto, a *serrano* or Indian from the highlands, together with a friend Crispin, tries to help his sister who is struggling to survive in Chimbote. But none of them escapes degradation. The agony Arguedas feels on hearing the Indians exchange their habits, language and songs for a peculiarly debased Spanish can finally be accommodated only in the vast sexual metaphor of the *zorra*, the vixen which engulfs as well as confuses, the bay of Chimbote open like the whores who surround it. This metaphor, notably in the climactic end to chapter 3 (a ritual act of cunnilingus in a night club-brothel), comes to stand as the only informing principle among a mass of detail and increasingly elusive characters. More crucially it quite eclipses that of the *zorros*, the authorial foxes. On page 100 Arguedas asks himself what the foxes are doing in the book; by page 211 he admits they are out of sight.

At the outset of the novel it had after all been the foxes who, lapsing into Quechua, had set the scene and promised to control it. They did this as privileged creatures, able to diagnose hidden sickness, like Tamtañamca's, and as supreme representatives of the two main regions of traditional Peru, the Andes and the coast. In his novel, Arguedas emphasizes their etiological importance, and stresses their ability to understand the 'real' underlying moral and economic geography of Peru, encouraged by their common preference for the hero from Above, Huatyacuri, over his rival from Below. But the foxes vanish and, with them, the serpent *amaru* whom they themselves say 'will not end', as well as those characters in the novel who appear as possible modern counterparts to Huatyacuri (Crispin and Asto, for example). Extraordinarily enough, and even at a formal level, this 'fading out' is anticipated in the original Quechua narrative. After the Fox from Above has told the story of Tamtañamca, his companion from Below says that 'down there' things are far worse. He gives a few shocking details, though hints that a cure may be possible there too. We never know what this 'cure' may be, however, because being 'too long for now', the fox's story is left for 'another time', and in fact is not to be found in the Quechua text. We are left in suspense, just as we are by Arguedas's own incomplete novel.

It is as if the idea of the foxes occurred to Arguedas at the end of the devastating First Diary, as a controlling device which had in it the paradox and the risk of his own situation. For his purposes the authority of this 'classic' Quechua text could never be as 'safe' as the *Popol vuh* was for Asturias. The very evanescence of the foxes is made into a token of their being alive still. Arguedas says that, though they are beyond his personal reach, they go on 'looking and learning'. So doing, of course, they can by implication 'see through' him, their 'wise' author. The extent that he demeans himself as the author of this last work can be disconcerting. For while (with Roa Bastos) he has come immeasurably closer to another, threatened America than any other Latin American writer, he also cast doubt in his very last diary entries on his own moral position, and said he actually regretted his inadequate 'technique', his first provincial love.

But this humility is deceptive, like the whole apparent artlessness of the book. For his suicide and the abrupt end of the book can be understood as an artistic gesture, the atonement for inadequacy he sensed in himself, maybe, but one which necessarily reinforces values against which such inadequacy can be measured.

He would not merely witness Tupac Amaru's agony. This would explain the paradoxical confidence, faith in eventual triumph, of his correspondence in Quechua during the very last weeks of his life with Hugo Blanco, the imprisoned guerrilla leader, who addressed him as father: 'taytay José María'.[12] It would suggest a less pathetic end for the story of Guimarães Rosa's which haunts him throughout *The Fox from Above and the Fox from Below*. This is 'The Third Bank of the River' ('O tercer margem do rio'), in which a man sacrifices everything in order to keep a silent and lonely vigil between the two banks of a wide river, enduring all hazard in his narrow canoe as if 'suspended in its mirror smoothness'; his last and only words are his salute to his son, who promises to take his place, before in fact failing in courage and disappearing among the trees.

MARIO VARGAS LLOSA

The colonel almost swallowed the mike but he didn't know
where to begin so he squeaked, 'Cadets!' and rested a
while and squeaked, 'Cadets!' and his voice cracked, I
laughed out loud, you bitch, with everyone stock-still and
silent, shaking in their boots. Okay, Skimpy, do you know
what he said, I mean besides squeaking, 'Cadets! Cadets!
Cadets!', we'll settle all these problems among ourselves,
just a few words to beg indulgence in the name of everyone,
of you, of the officers, for myself, our most humble apologies,
and the woman she got five minutes applause, they say she
started crying with emotion seeing us bashing our palms to
applaud her and she started throwing kisses at everybody,
too bad she was so far away. I couldn't tell if she was ugly
or good looking, young or old. Didn't that make shivers run
down your spine, Skimpy, when he said 'Third Year, dress
uniforms. Fourth and Fifth, as you were.' You know why
nobody made a move, not the officers, the noncoms, the
brigadiers, the guests, not even the Dogs? because the
devil really exists. And then she burst out, 'Colonel' and he
said, 'My dear lady', because she was the ambassador's wife,
everyone stirred, but what's happening, 'I beg you, Colonel',
'I'm at a loss for words,' 'Sir, not into the mike,' 'I beseech
you, Colonel,' how long did it last, Skimpy? Not long,
everybody was looking at fatty and the mike and the woman,
all talking at once and when she spoke we realized she was
a *gringa*. 'As a personal favour to me, Colonel?' There was a
dead silence, everyone at attention. 'Cadets! Cadets! We'll
forget this shameful incident, let it never happen again,
you know the punishment you deserve but this gracious
and distinguished lady,' and he bowed to her, 'is your
champion.' They say Gamboa said afterwards 'Is this a

goddamned nunnery, women giving orders in the barracks,'
so show your appreciation, who could re-create the cheering
of the school, a locomotive starting out slow, chug, one two
three four five, chug, one two three four, chug, one two
three, chug, one two, chug, one, chug, chug, chugchugchug,
and over again to chug-chug-chug, and over again, and the
ones from the Guadaloupe were sore as hell at our sports
day performance and we went chug-chug-chug, we also had
to give the ambassador's wife our hooray, hoorah, even the
Dogs began applauding, the officers and the noncoms, don't
stop, go on, chug-chug-chug, keep your eyes on the colonel,
the ambassador's wife and the minister start leaving, the
minister turns back and says, you think you're all pretty
smart but I'm going to wipe the floor with you, but he began
to laugh, and General Mendoza, and the ambassadors and
the officers and the guests too, chug-chug-chug, we're
the best in the world, hooray, hoorah, chug-chug-chug, the
cadets of the Leoncio Prado one hundred percent, hooray
for Peru, Cadets, one day our land will call us and we'll be
there, stouthearted and highminded, 'Where's that
Gambarina so I can kiss him on the mouth?' Jaguar said,
I mean if he's still alive after the bouncing I gave him, the
woman was sobbing with the cheers, Skimpy, life in the
Academy is hard and strict but it's got its compensations, too
bad the Circle never got back to what it was, the devil
always sticks his filthy nose into everything, I used to feel
great when the thirty of us got together in the latrine, so
now we're going to get screwed on account of that peasant
Cava, on account of a lousy pane of glass, for Christ's sake
get your teeth out of me, Skimpy, you bitch.

La ciudad y los perros (Barcelona 1963).
Translated by Lysander Kemp as *The Time of the Hero*
(London 1966); translation here considerably revised.
Chapter 3

The open day at Leoncio Prado, a military school in Lima, has
been saved from chaos at the last moment by the onslaught of
officers beating the boys into order with the buckle ends of their

belts. The boys are saved from further punishment by the intervention of the ambassador's wife (identified as a *gringa* or 'white
woman' from the north), and the occasion ends in driving applause.

The disorder has been an opportunity for the violence endemic
in the school to explode, and for the military discipline of the
place to be publicly swamped by the swelling enthusiasm of the
cadets. For below the official code, which itself is brutal enough,
seethes their world with its own taboos, hierarchies and com-
pulsions, these being more coercive in the formation of all the
cadets. They inhabit a Darwinian jungle in which the weak cannot avoid being victims, and in which the strong, the larger lads
of the final year, give free rein to the less agreeable human in-
stincts. At the very top stands the Jaguar, the leader of the Circle,
a terrorist group which had enjoyed complete power within the
larger official structure before one of them, 'the peasant (*serrano*)
Cava', was expelled from the school for stealing an examination
paper (the evidence being 'a lousy pane of glass'). Boa, the speaker
of the passage, has been another member; and although he feels
their finest days must be past, they continue to make themselves
felt; here Jaguar has distinguished himself by laying into Gamboa,
the fairest and least corruptible of the officers, whom they refer
to by the insultingly feminine name Gambarina.

The standard activities of the Circle include collective masturba-
tion (stimulus being provided by pornography written by Alberto,
one of their number); assault, which becomes murder when the
'Slave', Ricardo Arana, is suspected by them of having denounced
Cava; buggery, a speciality of Curly's, who selects well-rounded
first-years with the air of a connoisseur; and bestiality, the partners
being hens and llamas, and in the chronic case of Boa, a scraggy
bitch called Skimpy, to whom he confides his innermost experiences, as here. Normally this subculture flourishes, not just un-
hindered but effectively fostered by official attitudes in the
school. Cava's expulsion resulted from the Circle's straying beyond
the accepted limit and challenging an official code with which it
otherwise gets along more or less harmoniously. The *machismo* of
the place is so deeply ingrained that even after the fiasco of the
open day, the highest in command are easily drawn into the mass
enthusiasm of their pupils and find common idols in the honour of
school and country.

Vargas Llosa has said of the two years he spent at Leoncio Prado (which exists, and under that name) that they marked him, probably for life. He began to write his accounts of his dog's life there (the Spanish title means 'The city and the Dogs' – a slang word for the cadets) shortly after leaving. The eventual publication of his book caused some scandal; and the authorities of Leoncio Prado felt personally affronted enough to burn a thousand copies publicly in the yard of the school. Vargas Llosa speaks of all his work as the product of personal experience, and to this extent *The Time of the Hero* undoubtedly began as revenge and an exorcism; as Boa says 'the devil really exists'. However it is the opposite of a diatribe: true to another rule of his code as a writer he has completely effaced himself from the novel as a character. This is not to say that anyone familiar with stories of Vargas Llosa's life, as he himself has told them, would not find autobiographical elements in it, beyond the fact that Leoncio Prado was his school. The memories of home and family recorded by Ricardo Arana, the Slave shot dead to avenge Cava, coincide in more than one point with Vargas Llosa's own. He came to Lima from the north of Peru, an only child spoilt by mother and aunts, who resented his errant father's return to the family on their move to the capital. The life of Jaguar in the rougher quarters of that town became well-known to Vargas Llosa as an older boy, and provided the substance of his first book, *The Chiefs* (*Los jefes*, 1959), a collection of short stories. Again, as one who earned ambiguous respect for his early talent for writing salacious literature, Alberto resembles his author to some degree. But this is the point: if Vargas Llosa inhabits his work, it is after fragmenting himself beyond all possibility of singular recognition. To have done otherwise would have defeated his purpose: 'If the reader spies the author intervening, acting vicariously, crouching behind his characters, the fiction crumbles, because it means that these beings are not free and that the reader's freedom is not being respected either, that the author wants him as an accomplice in contraband, wants to impress on him ideas and beliefs made digestible as facts.'[1]

This stringent authorial proposition demands a stringent dialectical mechanism, in the terms of Lukács, or Vargas Llosa's own mentor Sartre. And the way his characters move in a structure of evident complexity is worth looking at. The narrative falls into two parts, which hinge on the murder of Arana; this is a crucial act which threatens the self-sufficiency of the school's code, its capacity to regulate itself. Though the attempt to hush it up eventually succeeds, the two separate worlds of the novel, that of Peru's citizens and that of the 'dogs', are brought together by it, as they are, less gravely, when visitors from outside (General Mendoza, the ambassador's wife and so on) attend Leoncio Prado on open day and both affect and are affected by what happens there. But the two parts of the novel do not correspond to these two worlds. Rather, the eight chapters of each part are sub-divided into various narrative passages which run concurrently throughout and deal now with the school and now with life out-side it.

In these narrative passages we rarely hear an omniscient authorial voice and then it is used deliberately to 'set a scene', to give the 'factual' co-ordinates of time and space:

> When the morning wind bursts on to La Perla, pushing
> the fog towards the sea and scattering it, and the grounds of
> Leoncio Prado Military Academy grow clear like a smoke-
> filled room when the windows have just been opened, an
> anonymous soldier appears yawning in the doorway of the
> soldiers' barracks and walks towards the cadets' quarters
> rubbing his eyes.

Otherwise the narratives are each concerned with a given number of characters, whose thoughts and actions are recorded in the first or the third person, or in a 'stream of consciousness'. In this way the reader pieces together the histories, in the town and the school, of the main characters: Ricardo Arana the Slave, whose existence is relegated to the perfect tense; Alberto Fernandez, the 'poet' from well-to-do Miraflores, whose passages are appropri-ately slick and self-aware; Jaguar, further from a bourgeois illusion of individualism, is ostensibly more 'objective', though it is hard to detect before the dénouement that this ferocious leader of the Circle in the school is the same person as the firmly anonymous younger lad we see in the city: likeable, underprivileged, child-hood friend to Teresa (later Arana's, then Alberto's girl, and finally Jaguar's wife), and in his own way a slave.

Of these main characters, Boa, the confidant of the bitch Skimpy, is unique in belonging only to the school, outside which he does not articulately exist. His narrative passages are a major technical achievement of the novel. He was born at a late stage in the drafting when Vargas Llosa felt that by recreating his own experience in a set of rigorously independent characters he had weakened its original psychic (if not visceral) charge. In particular, he found that the more obviously 'shocking' aspects of life there, the buggery and bestiality and so forth, were hard to convey without lapses into pornography, or in any case into a kind of prose which obstructed what he was wanting to say. After several experiments he got the idea of Boa: he is a ubiquitous eye, a 'protoplasmic' entity contained by the school (to and by which he is effectively confined), who registers experience without even the implicit need for judgement, sequence, or logic. His thoughts are grammatically fluid and wholly unexplained, a sort of 'consciousness without consciousness' as the Peruvian critic J. M. Oviedo has put it.[2]

As if independently of him as speaker, through his words we get a special 'inner' sense of the general excitement at Leoncio Prado's open day. For example, when we learn from the phrases he repeats that the colonel was encouraged not actually to announce that he was at a loss for words, it is we, not Boa, who construct the joke by remembering the colonel's earlier inadequacy at the microphone. Similarly, when Boa says he couldn't see whether or not the ambassador's wife was 'good-looking' having regretted he was so far from the kisses she blew, once again it is the reader who puts together what, strictly speaking is not even a train of associations for Boa. These qualities of his speech allow us to 'read' him yet more fully. Boa's amorality causes the professional integrity of the abused officer Gamboa to emerge as such, for Gamboa is the only person who objects to the wilful intrusion from outside into a problem of internal order ('Is this a goddamned nunnery. women giving orders in the barracks'). Indeed, this is actively reinforced by Boa's failure to recognize the implications of his blind enthusiasm. As a *gringa*, a powerful emissary from the north who can ask 'personal favours' from a virtually subject nation, the ambassador's wife gives a glimpse of the status vis-à-vis the U.S.A. not just of the school but of most Latin American nations. With great mastery on Vargas Llosa's part (for none of this is the least obtrusive in the text) Boa is made to expose, like Faulkner's Benjy, what might be called the mentality of a situation, as well as the darker areas of the human psyche.

As the most instinctual of the creatures in *The Time of the Hero* Boa has a fundamental importance. His narratives tell us most about the school as a microcosmic jungle. For to Boa are given the most bestial and potentially obscene episodes, saliently the buggering of a hen and a sadistic assault of Curly's, which previously Vargas Llosa had found most awkward to narrate. These two episodes were eventually fused in Boa's recorded thoughts at the end of chapter 1; the grossest words and acts are not shocking or diverting merely, but manifestations of a brutality where chopper and abused flesh are part of the same undeniable metaphor and exist within the same Vicious Circle:

> The Jaguar was on the lavatory, straining, and it looked as if he was being screwed. How about it, Jaguar, how about it? Shut up, they're cutting me, I've got to concentrate. And the beak? And suppose we buggered the fatboy, Curly said. Who? The one in the ninth, the fatboy. Haven't you ever pinched him? Oomph. It isn't a bad idea. but does he let you or doesn't he? They tell me Lañas buggers him when he's on guard duty. Oomph, at last. How about it, the bastard said. And who goes first, I don't want to do it now with all the noise she makes. Here's a piece of string for her beak. Don't let her go, peasant, or she'll fly away.

In the open-day episode Boa's excitement with Skimpy is less acute (less orgasmic), but the underlying associations between sexual and military aggression are the same, as is the suggestion that in Boa's world sexual encounters can only be a violation. Warning the bitch to be careful with her teeth, Boa relives the excitement of the collective cheers ('don't stop, go on') which made the *gringa* 'sob', intensely involved with the animal partner at whom his monologues are directed.

The greater the excitement, the harder it is to tell exactly what psyche Boa gives us access to. His chanted 'chugs' are those of a hysteria beyond social control or formulation. Indeed while he solved one problem in the creation of *The Time of the Hero*, Boa implicitly raises others, by so effectively transcending the careful structuring of the novel, into areas, classes, groups and characters whose identity is socio- sooner than psychological. It is therefore worth noting, in the opening passage of quotation, how purpose-fully Vargas Llosa goes on to recall Boa from the jungle into his social environment, in phrases which appear almost too con-sciously satirical:

> we're the best in the world, hooray, hoorah, chug-chug-chug, the cadets of Leoncio Prado one hundred percent, hooray for Peru, Cadets, one day our land will call us and we'll be there. . .

Except for this possible ambiguity in Boa, an over-reliance on coincidence in the use of Teresa as the girl friend of the cadets, and irritating features like the perversely late disclosure that Jaguar was Teresa's childhood friend, *The Time of the Hero* is a highly accomplished first novel. Vargas Llosa showed great power of orchestration in the way he opposed and integrated the two worlds of the novel (the school and the city), and registered a situation, in the Sartrean sense, in order to define 'its' rather than 'his' characters. In his next novel, *The Green House* (*La casa verde*, 1966), he went on to encompass vaster and more diverse material. The two geographical 'nodes' of this book are Piura, a town in northern Peru where Vargas Llosa lived before the family moved to Lima, and Santa Maria de Nieves in the Amazon area of the country, unknown to him before he went there in 1958 in the company of an anthropologist. In so far as he now incorporates larger tracts of territory into his novel and so writes on an overtly national scale, it is notable that the middle gets left out: the traditional heartland of the Andes or Sierra (whose capital Cuzco means navel in Quechua). We recall how, in *The Time of the Hero*, Cava had not just seemed inept and provincial as a *serrano*, but had actually been removed (expelled) at an early stage in the plot. This implies no lack of interest in that part of Peru's culture which had captivated so many novelists before him. Like his friend Arguedas, to whom he has expressed deep allegiance, Vargas Llosa spent much of his childhood in the Andean area: he was born in Arequipa, and went to school in Cochabamba (Bolivia) before coming 'down' to Piura and Lima.[3] But it does suggest that he has not found the world of the highland Quechua adaptable to his concerns and technique as a novelist. By contrast, the kinds of social and economic structure on which he lays such emphasis may be detected much more readily in the Amazon area, in many respects a dependency of the coast and the capital.

Piura, the first of the two settings in *The Green House*, is described in narrative passages which derive once again from Vargas Llosa's adolescent experience[4] (the overall structure being very similar to that of his first novel). One of these passages tells the story of the legendary forerunner of the present brothel in the town, an unpretentious one-roomed 'green house' (so painted; green has sexual connotations in Spanish), with musicians and drink, and space for the couples outside in the surrounding dunes under the stars. Another sequence deals with the district in the town called the 'mangachería', home of a tough community of 'Unconquerables' who lived beyond the control of the police (another brood of 'chiefs'), and whose distinction it was to be keen supporters of the fascist 'Unión revolucionaria' party in Peru. The sequences set in Santa Maria de Nieves and its jungle surroundings have as their subjects: the despotic Fushia (historically Tushia), a criminal Japanese who after the Second World War created a vast empire by brutality and force among the Huambisa and Aguaruna Indians; the socially enlightened Jum, brutally tortured for his attempts to establish a co-operative among the Indians as a defence against gross exploitation by Fushia and the rubber traders; and some nuns who acquire pupils for their missionary school by having Indian girls stolen from their families, and who effectively train them simply to be either maid or mistress to the coastal bourgeoisie. Though grotesque, this trade in nun-trained Indians between the jungle and the coast, the wilds and the known world, provides one of the narrative links which enable Vargas Llosa to use structure alone to tell his story. At any event, on entering the jungle areas of his novel we find no equivalent of the *individual* explorers who served as the heroes and the narrative threads of *The Lost Steps* and *The Vortex*.

The narratives or stories and their respective settings in *The Green House* are made to complement and interanimate each other by techniques like those of the first novel, except that now everything is on a much grander scale and chronology itself becomes less stable, notably because of unannounced flashbacks *within* given sequences and dialogues. From the very first sentences (which deal with one of the missionary expeditions to round up Indian girls) the reader is thrust into a dense atmosphere whose luxuriance is never idle, rich in plot and hardly relieved by paragraph division. In this work Vargas Llosa gives most evidence of his admiration of the high moments of the European chivalresque novel, notably the Catalan *Tirant lo blanc*, which he has championed as a critic,[5] with its vivid and impartial realism. In many respects *The Green House* may be thought of as a good adventure story, this being a description which certainly fits his subsequent 'jungle novel' *Pantaleon and the Whores* (*Pantaleon y las visitadoras*, 1973). Indeed, one criticism of *The Green House* has been for its apparently simple concern with action and with surfaces, however many-faceted. There is little of the interiorization of character found in *The Time of the Hero*, and no equivalent of Boa's central consciousness. Fushia, for example, manifold in action and appearance, remains enigmatic, so that the devices used in the earlier novel to join disparate episodes and scenes come under more strain, and in one case really do fail to work. Lituma in the jungle is an associate of Fushia's, a hardened soldier at one with the code of the place he inhabits. On his arrival in Piura he is reported to have been one of the Unconquerables, and founder of the first legendary brothel there; but he is so sadly changed on his 'return', so gratuitously meek and careful of his wife's welfare, that he seems incredible as a single 'personality'. The kind of disjunction visible in Jaguar, between his being in the city and his being in the school, recurs here in the second novel, exacerbated by the greater power of the two worlds, or 'continents' as they have been called, of the book.

For this and other reasons Vargas Llosa's third novel, *Conversation in The Cathedral* (*Conversación en la Catedral*, 1969), should be understood as the unified achievement of ambitions separately realized in his previous works. This novel has a palpable psychic centre and is vast in compass and scale (the sheer size of its four books could not be accommodated in a single volume and it is published in two). Taking as a first point of reference a character unmistakably like Boa in his instinctuality and his visceral, a-logical perception, Vargas Llosa constructs not just a school and its municipal counterparts in Lima, but the whole of life in Odría's Peru (1948–56) as he knew it. It is true that this ambition is embryonic in *The Time of the Hero*. The 'representative' quality of most of the characters in that book is clear: Cava, the *serrano* or peasant raw from the hills; Jaguar, a member of the urban working-class fighting for survival; Alberto, the bourgeois son from Miraflores, who later compromises only too readily with the U.S.-protected habits of his class. And more than once the moral economy of the school is openly equated with larger structures, crucially in the extensive white-washing and public silencing of the murder of Arana, the slave-victim. But the links between school and city are not sufficiently articulated to convey collusion of any intimacy or on any scale. Above all, Boa's 'central' consciousness has to be confined to the school. The result is that the reader cannot be sure (there being of course no internal reason why he should expect to be), what it is that the school is a microcosm of: whether it is the human condition; *machismo* as arrested adolescence with deep roots in sexuality (of the kind exposed in the remarkable novella *The Cubs* (*Los cachorros*, 1967); a particular area of Latin American society at a given historical moment; or an uncertain amalgam of all these things.

If Boa resembles Ambrosio, the central speaker in *Conversation in The Cathedral*, it is as an underprivileged forerunner. Ambrosio dominates the prose of the later novel, though still with the 'unconscious consciousness' of his predecessor. The four hours of his conversation (in the bar called The Cathedral) give an increasingly intricate awareness of the eight years of Odría's dictatorship and of large areas of Peru during that period. The narrative 'pyramid' which emerges has been meticulously described by Oviedo, with diagrams and tables and with Ambrosio at the apex; and its sheer mass of detail resists any possible summary here. There can be little doubt about Vargas Llosa's achievement: it is the one big work in his life as a novelist in which he can feel himself duly exhausted, which has stretched his huge imaginative energy to palpable limits. Unlike other Latin American 'dictatorship' novels (Asturias's *The President* for example) *Conversation in The Cathedral* draws not at all on reservoirs of violence and fear, and is wholly immune to the myths of nightmare. Vargas Llosa's Odría thrives on minute daily corruption and duplicity, to which our unerring and unquestioning witness is Ambrosio, chauffeur, servant, bodyguard and confidant. This regime (which provoked no heroic resistance) is held responsible by Vargas Llosa for the 'theft' perpetrated on him and his contemporaries, in a situation considerably more complex than that of Leoncio Prado, finally an isolated symptom of Odría's military origins and code.

That Vargas Llosa should implicitly so revenge himself in literature without lapsing into invective, or breaking the spell of his invented reality, is a measure of his stature as a novelist, which is comparable with that of the realist giants of nineteenth-century Europe.[6] But his very self-effacement and his attention to structure at the expense of character and individual psychology alert us to ambiguities in his novels which he himself has discussed. Though his characters are autonomous in the sense that they are not authorial masks or guide-narrators, they are nonetheless subjected to forces stronger than themselves. As we have seen, Jaguar and Lituma are fragmented as characters by the structures of the novels to which they belong. The difficulty is to know how far, in Vargas Llosa's invented reality, these forces correspond to facts of a truly socio-economic order and how far they are fated and beyond man's control. This is the question raised by Boa, in so far as his atavistic urges can no longer be contained in or explained by the school as a social microcosm; by the gratuitous cruelty of the magnate Fushia, who often appears more psychopathic than simply 'feudal'; and by the utter and insistent degradation of which Ambrosio, in his turn, is representative. Implicit in all this is the old problem of the innermost nature of man, which Rousseau, as a first premise in his social contract, claimed need not be evil, and which Cortázar approached via the psychological route of Sade. For his part, Vargas Llosa has expressed the unsettling suspicion that the highest function of the novel may be merely to exorcise the past and to offer vicarious satisfaction, with its appearance of cohesion, in a world that remains unredeemable. Further, he has said that great novels will flourish exactly 'when reality ceases to have precise meaning for a historic community'.[7] What he modestly omits to mention is that he is one of the few Latin American novelists who have succeeded in conveying a developed sense of such a historic community.

GABRIEL GARCÍA MÁRQUEZ

Many years later, as he faced the firing squad, Colonel Aureliano Buendía was to remember that distant afternoon when his father took him to discover ice. At that time Macondo was a village of twenty adobe houses, built on the bank of a river of clear water that ran along a bed of polished stones, which were white and enormous, like prehistoric eggs. The world was so recent that many things lacked names, and in order to indicate them it was necessary to point. Every year during the month of March a family of ragged gypsies would set up their tents near the village, and with a great uproar of pipes and kettledrums they would display new inventions. First they brought the magnet. A heavy gypsy with an untamed beard and sparrow hands, who introduced himself as Melquíades, put on a bold public demonstration of what he himself called the eighth wonder of the learned alchemists of Macedonia. He went from house to house dragging two metal ingots and everybody was amazed to see pots, pans, tongs, and braziers tumble down from their places and beams creak with the desperation of nails and screws trying to emerge, and even objects that had been lost for a long time appeared from where they had been searched for most and went dragging along in turbulent confusion behind Melquíades's magical irons. 'Things have a life of their own,' the gypsy proclaimed with a harsh accent. 'It's simply a matter of waking up their souls.' José Arcadio Buendía, whose unbridled imagination always went beyond the genius of nature and even beyond miracles and magic, thought that it would be possible to make use of that useless invention to extract gold from the bowels of the earth. Melquíades, who was an honest man, warned him: 'It won't work for that.' But José Arcadio Buendía at

that time did not believe in the honesty of gypsies, so he
traded his mule and a pair of goats for the two magnetized
ingots. Úrsula Iguarán, his wife, who relied on those
animals to increase their poor domestic holdings, was
unable to dissuade him. 'Very soon we'll have gold enough
and more to pave the floors of the house,' her husband
replied. For several months he worked hard to demonstrate
the truth of his idea. He explored every inch of the region,
even the riverbed, dragging the two iron ingots along and
reciting Melquíades's incantation aloud. The only thing he
succeeded in doing was to unearth a suit of fifteenth-
century armour which had all of its pieces soldered together
with rust and inside which there was the hollow resonance
of an enormous stone-filled gourd. When José Arcadio
Buendía and the four men of his expedition managed to
take the armour apart, they found inside a calcified skeleton
with a copper locket containing a woman's hair around
its neck.

Cien años de soledad (Buenos Aires 1967).
Translated by Gregory Rabassa as *One Hundred Years
of Solitude* (New York 1970). Chapter 1.

Earliest memories of García Márquez's imaginary Macondo are
prehistoric, like the polished egg-like stones of its river. The
town was founded, at an uncertain date, somewhere deep in the
swamps of northern Colombia, by Colonel Aureliano's father,
José Arcadio Buendía, after a long and arduous flight from the
known world and his own past. He and Úrsula Iguarán, first
cousins, were the first pair in this early world; they constructed
the town and effectively arranged the lives of the people who
came with them from the coast. The fortunes of the family they
engendered, seven generations in all, give the book its thread and
its title. Melquíades and his gypsies, ragged as they are, burst into
the solitude of Macondo as men wiser and older than its founding
family.

As the characters in *One Hundred Years of Solitude* themselves
remark, events in Macondo seem often to repeat themselves, in
apparent defiance of historical sequence. The very names of the

characters, repeated from generation to generation (there are no fewer than four José Arcadios), reinforce this impression, which is created in the skilful vagueness of the opening sentences. Phrases like 'many years later', and 'that distant afternoon' lead back through the prehistoric stones to a timeless world where (in an allusion to Carpentier and his magic realism) we are told many things still needed to be named. Though a genealogical thread runs from the first José Arcadio and Úrsula to the ill-fated last scion of the family, the novel, divided into twenty sections of near-equal length, retains an episodic feeling. Many of the characters and events were familiar to García Márquez's readers before its appearance. Almost all his published work before *One Hundred Years of Solitude* is, or could be, set in Macondo and presents people from that town or who have to do with it. *Leaf Storm* (*La hojarasca*, 1955) deals at length with the banana boom there, which surfaces again in the thirteenth and fourteenth chapters of *One Hundred Years of Solitude*. The lonely unrewarded hero of *No-one Writes to the Colonel* (*El coronel no tiene quien le escriba*, 1961) closely resembles Colonel Aureliano Buendía himself, whom, we are told, he served during the civil wars. In *The Evil Hour* (*La mala hora*, 1961), Macondo suffers the deluge again described in the later novel, while his short stories, collected in part in *Big Mama's Funeral* (*Los funerales de la Mamá Grande*, 1962), are vignettes of life in the town. In this sense the novel can be understood as a comprehensive gesture, the gathering into one context of moments hitherto existing separately. Macondo itself was the name of a plantation near the small town (Aracataca) on Colombia's Caribbean coast where García Márquez grew up. As the location of his various narratives he has shaped and populated it from the stories told to him by his grand-parents, in whose house he lived as a child. In the novel, Úrsula, the mother and grandmother of all, is defined by her ability to recall and recount lives and situations otherwise threatened with oblivion or confusion.

The gypsies' visit was an experience Macondo could take, though José Arcadio is crazed with greed, wanting to tear gold like iron from Arcadia's breast. The gypsies' intrusion into the fairy-tale world of early Macondo is the first of many such intrusions, which present the question of the town's moral location.

The gypsies are followed by the *corregidor* Moscote, sent by the central government, whose presence there is at first manifestly absurd but becomes normal, even necessary. There follows a series of secular and religious officials, vigilantes and surveyors carried in by ever-improved communications with the outside world. Even potent emblems of pre-temporal existence like those enormous polished stones in Macondo's river are pulverized, almost unnoticed, when José Arcadio II goes ahead with his scheme to build a canal connecting Macondo with the coast. Like the Sulaco of Conrad's *Nostromo* (which also lived through 'a hundred years' of isolation), the town Macondo itself thus acquires a special significance in the space and time of the novel, a significance García Márquez's beguiling prose neither highlights nor denies.

One Hundred Years of Solitude has been sold and read so widely in Latin America, and has been taken so very much to heart there, as to support the idea that Macondo might be exemplary of Latin America as a whole, a luminous chronicle of a special condition. And it is true that García Márquez contrives brilliantly to attribute to the town an experience both local and precise and more broadly characteristic. The hundred lonely years recounted in the novel would thus begin more or less with the (nominal) political independence won by the states of Latin America in the nineteenth century, and bring us up to modern times. To attempt to synthesize so much historical experience within a single novel is clearly an ambitious project, undertaken by few other Latin American novelists. Carpentier, in *The Lost Steps*, is one of them, and this must explain the frequent and not very flattering references to him.

Proceeding by categories, we may first note the imperial European presence symbolized in the fifteenth-century Spanish copper locket opened by José Arcadio, with the hair of a distant woman inside it, and (a few pages later in the same chapter) in the proud galleon stranded miles from the main (a virtuoso description of García Márquez's):

> When they woke up, with the sun already high in the
> sky, they were speechless with fascination. Before them,
> surrounded by ferns and palm trees, white and powdery

in the silent morning light, was an enormous Spanish
galleon. Tilted slightly to starboard, it had hanging from
its intact masts the dirty rags of its sails in the midst of its
rigging, which was adorned with orchids. The hull, covered
with an armour of petrified barnacles and soft moss, was
firmly fastened into a surface of stones. The whole structure
seemed to occupy its own space, one of solitude and
oblivion, protected from the vices of time and the habits
of the birds. Inside, where the expeditionaries explored with
careful intent, there was nothing but a thick forest of
flowers.

Then comes a series of encounters with native Indian and
imported black populations, variously resolved. After that the
civil wars which ravaged Colombia and other Latin American
countries in the post-Independent period are caught in the classic
nineteenth-century struggles between liberals and conservatives
which occupy the second quarter of the book and bring Colonel
Aureliano close to death. Following a standard historical pattern,
this strife is succeeded by the intrusion of Anglo-Saxon or *gringo*
interests, epitomized in Macondo by Mr Brown and the banana
growers, who exploit the local workers brutally. The whole condition of Macondo could initially be understood as that of a
hinterland beyond rivers and ports, 'where the sun smiles and
the seasons teem in vain, unseen and unenjoyed', its 'innocent'
posture being that of a continent or subcontinent until recently
at the mercy of purveyors of ideas and magnets from older parts
of the planet.

This historical dimension undoubtedly exists in the novel,
though things are more complicated, for Macondo and its inhabitants were never truly innocent. Moreover, García Márquez
appears less interested in displaying it for its own sake or his
reader's amusement than in having it there as something to play
against. History is compromised from the very start, as we have
seen, by the laying of those prehistoric eggs, and continues to be
by subtle distortions of time which culminate in Aureliano's and
our discovery that the wise Melquíades had foreseen what would
happen in Macondo and had written it down, in Sanskrit (his
mother tongue), on a sheaf of parchment. García Márquez also

shows that he doesn't want merely to chronicle the past by his admirably constant disregard of precise ages and dates. Situations throughout the book are leavened with more or less direct allusions to Biblical and other 'timeless' myths. Colonel Aureliano's sons are mysteriously murdered as if by an order of Herod, while a later, illegitimate, Aureliano is found in the bullrushes like Moses. Other events are neutralized temporally by a series of 'plagues': insomnia, dead birds raining from the sky, and so on. The greater the danger that a given event may seem to be historical, the stronger is García Márquez's mythical antidote: the banana company's massacre of thousands of strikers, for example, is followed by endless rain and a portentous flood, subsequently referred to as the Deluge, which washes away precise memory.[1] Down to the smallest detail, García Márquez's prose absorbs and loosens the possible intractability of a particular history. The words 'firing squad' in the opening sentence do not prompt us to wonder why or when Aureliano was facing it, any more than the 'gold' sought by José Arcadio specifically recalls the American substance which in history made his ancestors less amiably crazed with greed. Such potentially mythic terms sooner interact with each other, just below the surface of the narrative: 'father', 'ice', 'iron', 'bowels', 'earth'. On the other hand, the resonance they produce is never allowed to dehistoricize the narrative altogether. They are subject to the swift relating of events, and to an authorial superiority insinuated in phrases like 'useless invention', 'did not believe in the honesty of gypsies', 'the only thing he succeeded in doing'.

Our formal point of reference in this bemusing world of myth and history, even more than the place Macondo, is the Buendías' existence in it. From Aureliano's introductory memory of an afternoon spent with his father onwards, parochial genealogy acts as the guide to whatever larger message there is. The very founders of Macondo are José Arcadio's men, whose descendants exist only in so far as they have dealings with the Buendías. Later, García Márquez may convey brilliantly the sense of a moment in social and cultural history, in nineteenth-century bourgeois soirées round the pianola, for example, but in every case it is through the words, deeds and relationships of the family. We know about liberals of the period via the Colonel, and not as a party or group. Again, a mulatta like Nigromanta is introduced because the last Aureliano at one point needed a woman like her, not because the place had the remnants of a slave population. García Márquez even alerts us drily to his partiality. In the silly passions which involve the young Buendía girls Amaranta and Rebeca with Pietro Crespi, who is always in the family house as the pianola expert, there is a parody not just of their etiquette but of the bourgeois novel in the style of Isaac's *Maria* and of cameo description as a historiographical method. Similarly, Colonel Gerineldo Márquez's loyalty to the liberal cause is wrily equated with his personal devotion to Aureliano. Macondo exists only as long as the family tree flourishes there.

The family in turn owes its existence and its coherence to Úrsula,[2] their guardian. Her insight alone can detect the 'real' motives behind her offsprings' actions; her memory alone can retain their history and she alone can condone or condemn their acts. Her concern to restrain José Arcadio in his failure to respect 'nature' with his magnet is the first of several interventions which, at first ineffective, finally fulfil their purpose. By far the most dramatic of these is her hounding of the triumphant and resplendent Colonel Aureliano at one point during the civil war; she assaults him directly in front of his men and stops him from carrying out his plan of reprisals. She decides who is legitimate and who is not among her progeny. And she keeps them afloat financially with a private enterprise worthy of Mother Courage herself. By paying for and designing the house she provides a physical focus, and the further anyone strays from it the more blurred and less substantial they become. Precisely on her death, at the age of one hundred, not long before the ill-fated last scion of the tree is born and dies, things begin to fall apart, and the family's inner meaning is seriously exposed to question. The solitude of the title derives, then, not just from Macondo's physical isolation but from 'the solitary destiny' of the family itself, which she embodies more fully than anyone else.

Freakish things do happen in the Buendía family, for all Úrsula's surveillance and authority. There is more than one case of incest; and the last child of the line is born with a tail. Colonel Aureliano insists on marrying a girl who is not yet adolescent, and so small that she has to be lifted up to greet the wedding guests.

Some critics have made much of these and other oddities as examples of Macondo's fabulousness, and of its 'prelapsarian' inhabitants' way of living out Freudian fantasy, beyond taboo. Once again, this may be. But more to the point are the eminently normal Spanish-American ethics they otherwise adhere to. The men of the family may indulge their sexual urges ubiquitously, in scenes described with torrid zest by García Márquez. But the unmarried women either remain resolute virgins like Amaranta (Aureliano's sister), or get put into convents for indiscretion, leaving whores from outside the family, like Pilar Ternera, as social companions for the men. Ideals of man and womanhood are sharply distinguished; the men show unflinching courage in the face of violence and death, but are left to 'relieve their bellies' in the brothel run by Pilar Ternera, the Golden Boy, their only social centre. No untrammelled Eden, Macondo is strictly watched and influenced by Úrsula the matriarch, her ideal of the family being very like that traditionally revered in Colombia and other conservative Spanish-American countries.

Úrsula's injunctions are especially important in so far as they affect the family's racial and political attitudes. The early genera-tions of the family could hardly help coming into contact with the Guijara Indians and went as far as allowing one or two Buendía children to speak their language. But Úrsula's tacit resistance to them is soon confirmed: and they and their language are forgotten by everybody in a plague of amnesia which the Indians them-selves, conveniently enough, carry to the household. Again, the blacks, who appear 'out of nowhere', are assigned subservient roles as unquestioningly as they would have been anywhere in Colonial America. This subtle relegation of people there before Macondo's genesis or essential to its economy is always in favour of the Castilian blood flowing in José Arcadio's and Úrsula's veins. That suit of ancient Spanish armour dug up in the first chapter is a relic indeed, a palpable cult-object.

Translated from genealogy into history, the culture of Úrsula's family would no doubt appear oppressively reactionary and the obvious cause of their 'solitary destiny'. But this is a translation which García Márquez does not make as long as Úrsula exists as a living character in the novel. She may charm or disturb, but she is neither approved nor disapproved of. After her death it is another matter. Then she is held responsible for the 'pernicious vices' and the 'solitary calling' of the Buendías. And the last of the family line, Amaranta Úrsula and her nephew Aureliano earnestly hope that their child, the very last José Arcadio, can 'cleanse' them of this heritage since 'he was the only one in a century who had been engendered with love'. But this interpretation of Úrsula, as a kind of tropical Pedro Páramo,[3] belongs only to the three final chapters of the novel. As long as Úrsula lives, we are prevented from thinking too long about her as a creature of political and social consequence, by the bemusing qualities of García Márquez's prose. To return to the example of the family's relationship with the native Indians of their region: after the plague of amnesia they bring to the household, the Buendías try valiantly to cope, by naming the objects of their environment, affixing labels to them with accompanying explanations where necessary, as if to make it lexically habitable. Now besides being an extremely witty parody of Carpentier's notion that Latin Americans, Adamic or Arcadian, should busy themselves naming the things of their world as if it really was an unpopulated Eden, this passage reminds us yet again of the backwardness, isolation and racial exclusiveness of Macondo. But we don't dwell for a moment on the implications, politically, of all this. The event simply happens, and passes, and so do tragedies like the incessant civil war around the town or the terrible massacre of the plantation workers.

One Hundred Years of Solitude benefits, in its episodic, serial narration of events, from García Márquez's talents as a journalist–reporter (who had 'used Hemingway as an antidote to early readings of Faulkner')[4] and as a short story writer. The many luminous short stories about Macondo which preceded this novel, by virtue of their form and as a series of more or less marginal 'incidents', could avoid full confrontation with what García Márquez had made into the moral burden of his writing: the luxuriant and traumatic tropical world of Aracataca–Macondo. In his novels García Márquez could avoid this confrontation less easily, if only for formal reasons. The special achievements of *One Hundred Years of Solitude*, the best of these novels, may be gauged by reference to two previous ones: *Leaf Storm*, the first he published, and *The Evil Hour*, after which he remained silent for some time before producing *One Hundred Years of Solitude*.

García Márquez's principal achievement in *Leaf Storm* was the invention of Macondo, which though 'like' his birthplace, enjoyed an existence of its own, as Yoknapatawpha did for Faulkner and Santa Maria did for Onetti. There, in his account of the activities of the United Fruit Company during the banana boom and their effects on the local population, he had room to develop his skill at perceiving 'the intimate relationship which exists between the political–social structure of a given country and the behaviour of its inhabitants',[5] evident enough even in the separate and marginal incidents of his short stories. In the novel, however, this structure threatened to become too comprehensive and determinant, something which he himself, as another of its 'products', could not expect to escape from. As if to acknowledge this problem, the three Faulkneresque monologues which make up *Leaf Storm* (spoken by Isabel, her father the colonel, and her son) are brought to a close in the very year that the author was born (1928). Like the last José Arcadio in *One Hundred Years of Solitude* (born after Úrsula's death), he could thus at least intimate the notion of immunity from the historical and political processes observed in the novel. In *The Evil Hour*, his attempt to be 'equal' to, and to explain his heritage was more radical and overt. The intimate secrets of Macondo are exposed and analysed socially, by a device (the ubiquitous appearance in the town of *pasquinades*) which reveals the private thoughts of its inhabitants, about each other and themselves. This novel has been called a social and political 'x-ray' of the town, and in practice left García Márquez little opportunity to use his great story-telling talent. In their different ways, both novels attempted the same thing: to make sense of, in terms acceptable to a socially and politically conscious writer, and so to demystify, the amoral and overwhelming power of an inherited fable which holds him in thrall. In this respect the closing sentences of *The Evil Hour* are significant, with their reference to a 'new' possibility of liberation in Colombia and Latin America as a whole: 'The prison is full, but they say that the men are taking to the hills and that there are guerrilla groups everywhere.'

The main thing García Márquez went on to do in *One Hundred Years of Solitude* was apparently to forget this direct political

concern and personality to come to terms with Úrsula. He releases
her unconditionally as a narrative source, and no longer evaluates
in the same way the world which he and she share. Remembrance
of the massacre of strikers, so carefully analysed and assessed in
Leaf Storm, is now washed away by the rain so that the story of
the family can go on. The mesh of inner corruption in the town,
so excruciatingly probed in *The Evil Hour* is now surveyed with
bitter-sweet humour. It was this relaxation of focus which enabled
him to attempt his grand synthesis of Latin American experience.
By converting a family heritage into the narrative device of
genealogy, chronicle and myth, he made Macondo's boundaries
historically and geographically elastic. The evident success of this
new approach prompted some critics to reproach García Márquez
with loss of political faith, which they attributed specifically to
the reverses suffered by revolutionary and guerrilla movements
in Latin America in the 1960s, between the publication of *The
Evil Hour* and *One Hundred Years of Solitude*.[6] Whatever the
truth of this may be, *One Hundred Years of Solitude* can hardly
be considered a gesture of resignation. For García Márquez
exorcises Úrsula not by absolving or annihilating her but by
leaving her dead; he transfers the load to her living survivors.

The three chapters which come after Úrsula's death in the
novel are devoted to Amaranta Úrsula and Aureliano, and their
child José Arcadio. Now both parents, aunt and nephew, are
distinguished not just by this narrative 'orphanhood' but by a
moral independence from the family which few of their ancestors
have had. More than once, Amaranta Úrsula is said to be a
modern woman; she travels widely and on returning to Macondo
with her Belgian husband she momentarily looks as though she
can usurp her great-great-grandmother Úrsula as the woman of
the house. For his part, Aureliano acquires friends in the town, on
whom he comes to rely with an openness uncharacteristic of the
family, and who offer him in addition an entry to the 'universal'
world of literature and learning. The Catalan bookseller in the
town shares with him knowledge said rightly to be 'encyclopaedic', since it can situate Latin America as historically it was
first situated by the thinkers of the eighteenth century, and can
provoke an emancipation begun historically with the Wars of
Independence. The bookseller's own compositions become a

modern and less enslaving equivalent of the parchments of Melquíades, Macondo's first Old World visitor (the handwriting of both is said to be startlingly similar). Melquíades had predicted the destiny of the place by drawing on the wisdom of the ancients, in a Sanskrit embellished with signs of Greek and Roman authority ('He had composed it in Sanskrit, which was his mother tongue, and had ciphered the even lines with the personal mark of the Emperor Augustus and the odd lines with military marks of the Lacedemonians'). Having been 'determined' to translate Melquíades's version of his family's and Macondo's fate, Aureliano awakens to a larger and more immediate environment, and makes the acquaintance of other modern writers, among them the Colombian novelist Alvaro Cepeda (whom García Márquez met in Baranquilla, having left Aracataca), and the author himself. This is not the first time, in this Latin American novel, that we find an allusion to other Latin American novels: a certain colonel Lorenzo Gavilán had earlier been transferred, from active service in Mexico in Carlos Fuentes's account of the Mexican Revolution in *The Death of Artemio Cruz*, to join forces with the male Buendías as champions of the liberal cause in Colombia. And we have already noted the adroit parodies of Carpentier, and his philosophy of 'naming the things' of America; later, fun is made of the axiom that 'style is affirmed through history' (by now tantamount to anathema), and at one point we glimpse the tempestuous Victor Hugues himself, 'at sea' on the Caribbean and sailing for Guadeloupe – in the wrong direction (cf pp. 47–8). By the stage of the novel, however, at which 'Gabriel Márquez' himself appears as a character, with old Úrsula gone, this kind of reflexive illusion acquires added force and appears more necessary to the survival of a lone, orphaned figure like Aureliano.

The final chapter of *One Hundred Years of Solitude* announces itself as a finale, and suggests that Amaranta Úrsula and Aureliano cannot save their tribe (*estirpe*). The town and the house collapse around them, and for all their great love for each other, they cannot prevent everything falling apart in the last corruption of the atmosphere. Pilar Ternera's The Golden Boy – like the brothels in Santa Maria, Vargas Llosa's Piura and Arguedas's Cuzco, a place of relative enlightenment – is ceremonially shut for ever on her death at the age of 144. Amaranta Úrsula's Belgian husband, who travels abroad and for whom, as a result of a post-office error, Macondo has become confused with the Congo, almost gratefully breaks his bond with her on learning about Aureliano. The Catalan bookseller leaves, and as he fades into the distance urges his friends to do the same; except for Aureliano they do. His letters from Barcelona, like those of the character García Márquez from Paris (where the author actually went), become the couple's only link 'with the world'. And then that link is gone. The Catalan dies, and Gabriel Márquez is last seen writing in the room in which Oliveira's adoptive child 'Rocama-dour had died'. This is a reference to a moment in the Latin American novel to which Cortázar himself would later return in *Manuel's Book*, where the dead baby is resurrected, or at least for a time. García Márquez's elegant tribute to the integrity of the author of *Hopscotch* appeals to the reflexive power of literature, and serves as a redoubled presage.

For though the baby boy of Amaranta Úrsula and Aureliano is the first of the family to be engendered in love, the parents are too confined, genetically and otherwise, for the birth to 'cleanse' them of their heritage, as they had hoped it would. The mother dies in childbirth, and the last José Arcadio is born with the tail of a fabled creature, to be eaten alive by ants whose 'prehistoric' hunger reminds us of the implacable forces always latent in the stone eggs in Macondo's innocent-looking river. Thrown back entirely on himself, Aureliano can only think of going back to the parchments that will tell him his fate and from which the Catalan bookseller, and then love, had distracted him. With a tropical storm raging around him he reads ever more anxiously:

> Macondo was already a fearful whirlwind of dust and
> rubble being spun about by the wrath of the biblical
> hurricane when Aureliano skipped eleven pages so as not
> to lose time with facts he knew only too well, and he began
> to decipher the instant that he was living, deciphering it
> as he lived it, prophesying himself in the act of deciphering
> the last page of the parchments, as if he were looking into a
> speaking mirror. Then he skipped again to anticipate the
> predictions and ascertain the date and circumstances of his

death. Before reaching the final line, however, he had already understood that he would never leave that room, for it was foreseen that the city of mirrors (or mirages) would be wiped out by the wind and exiled from the memory of men at the precise moment when Aureliano Babilonia would finish deciphering the parchments, and that everything written on them was unrepeatable since time immemorial and forever more, because races condemned to one hundred years of solitude did not have a second opportunity on earth.

Aureliano Babilonia puts his last faith in the authority of Melquíades's ancient script: he is immured (*encastillado*) in literature, as in the tower of Babylon his name. Only in the scattering storm he discovers, like a persona of Borges, that such faith alone cannot save him. But because of the way in which the narrative, in crescendo, includes the reader in the act that Aureliano is performing (reading the reading), this realization of Aureliano's sweeps to its limit García Márquez's exposé of the novel as a literary object in a larger situation. The tropical storm tears away not just the leaves of the trees, as it does in Asturias's *Strong Wind* or had done in García Márquez's *Leaf Storm*, but those of the very idea of the book. This could be just a sophisticated example of the ability to use literature to make fun of people (*burlarse de la gente*) which Aureliano had discovered on meeting García Márquez and other friends in The Golden Boy. But it still 'opens' the novel to include and involve the reader, as Umberto Eco has defined that process,[7] in the way that Cortázar and José María Arguedas have done, each for his own reasons. Correspondingly, we move from the mode of exorcism of the past, with its secular load, to that of exhortation in the present. For, among the living, the last words can only be heard as a cry which demands its contradiction: 'they didn't have a second chance on earth'.[8]

A salient feature of the Latin American novel of the last thirty years has been the attempt to write about the subcontinent as a place with its own specific reality. Novelists with this aim have taken further the self-exploration begun in the nineteenth century, by the first realist writers of Latin America. From their early descriptions of bourgeois life in the coastal cities there was a gradual movement into the interior, a literary exploration of the unknown heart of the continent. With Asturias and Carpentier this exploration became a first priority, and for this reason their novels have been regarded as a common reference point by modern writers.

Asturias and Carpentier have appeared so important because of the historical and geographical scale of the reality they describe. In *Men of Maize*, Asturias gave access to a major culture, that of the Maya, which has survived from pre-Columbian times, and which owes little to Europe and its conventions, indeed to the Spanish language itself. At best his prose demonstrates that the ways of life and perceptions of the Maya, alien as they may appear, are no less valid than those imposed upon them since the time of the Spanish conquest. This feat alone greatly enriched the Latin American novel and may be considered a literary conquest of the first order.

In Carpentier's terms, the realm inhabited by Asturias's *Men of Maize* is part of the magic or marvellous reality of America, which it is the duty of every Latin American novelist to 'name' and describe. In Carpentier's own novels, however, pre-Columbian culture is only one of several ingredients, his tendency being always to grand synthesis. In *The Kingdom of this World*, *The Lost Steps* and *Explosion in a Cathedral* he returns again and again to those experiences which together may be said to define or characterize Latin American reality in nothing less than a global context. He has paid special attention to those revolutionary and emancipatory movements which had their origin in eighteenth-century Europe and which first fostered the very idea of an independent and self-sufficient Latin America. His narratives are more wide-ranging than Asturias's, and more erudite. Yet both authors may be thought of as pioneers of their own environment.

Fundamental as they are, Carpentier and Asturias are not without their limitations in the eyes of their contemporaries and successors. Perhaps the most important criticism made of their work concerns the nature of their involvement, as authors, in their 'subject matter'. Both venture far and deep into the unknown in their continent and present their readers with extraordinary trophies. But neither allows himself to linger in the world he has created, be it the forest of the Maya or of primeval South American Indians, or the 'gorgeous landscapes' of the Caribbean, America's inner sea. They withhold themselves, adopting baroque and sometimes ironic postures, and covertly guard their authorial consciousness outside the story and the concerns of its characters. This is so despite Asturias's genial solidarity with Gaspar Ilóm, the Maya hero of *Men of Maize*; and despite Carpentier's recognition that his protagonist Esteban might find a 'permanent home' in the inner land of America he sees in the vision in *Explosion in a Cathedral*. To this extent they appear as great American novelists for whom the moulding of geographical and historical experience, of the most diverse order, takes precedence over the situating of the self.

This is true of none of the other six novelists. With them, the position of the author within the novel becomes a matter of prime importance, and even becomes an explicit theme of the books they write, in the case of Onetti, Arguedas, Cortázar and García Márquez. There can be no doubt that this preoccupation with finding a place derives from a greater sense of social and political responsibility towards Latin America than is conveyed in the novels of Asturias and Carpentier. Between the setting of Onetti's novels, for instance, and that of Rulfo's there is an apparent recurrence of that antithesis between city and province stated at the beginnings of Latin American prose by Sarmiento. But these two settings now prove to be intimately alike. Santa Maria and

Comala, and indeed the Macondo of García Márquez's first novels, are all-encompassing realities. We enter them aware of the huge imaginative effort which has gone into their creation. By means of internal monologues in the style of Faulkner and complex presentations of character (Larsen; Preciado), Onetti and Rulfo create worlds in which the reader and the novelists themselves are necessarily implicated. This deep identification with the places and communities they have known in life makes them interestingly similar to the Scandinavian novelists of 'marginal' and lonely societies, whom they also concur in admiring. (It is curious to note that the protagonist of Knut Hamsun's *Hunger* compared his predicament with that of a 'man in South America'). They write about their particular parts of a quite unmarvellous America as witnesses to exploitation, solitude and decay. And by the very intensity of the atmospheres they build up they show too that to be merely a witness is in itself a major feat of courage and imagination.

The novels of Vargas Llosa are also novels of testimony. But we find, too, a new element: the will to exorcism. To perform this act Vargas Llosa makes social and political structure predominate over the psychology of the individual. These structures are urban in origin, and when Vargas Llosa writes about the jungle, as he does in *The Green House*, he does so by showing the wide-spread influence of the economy of the city. Unrivalled in his invention of a reality that is elaborate, self-sufficient and, by analogy, historically valid, Vargas Llosa emphasizes structure to the point of fragmenting the identity of individual characters, and of removing all trace of himself as author. In this, his discussion of the work of his friend García Márquez greatly illuminates his own. He refers to García Márquez as a 'deicide',[1] one for whom the independent reality of the novel matches and overcomes that of environment and personal heritage. He has suggested, too, that the vivid exterior surfaces of that neglected genre the chivalresque novel (*Tirant lo blanc*; *Amadis*) acted, as they did for him, as an antidote to intense psychological introspection. However, since he himself is absent, even as a source of moral value, Vargas Llosa, like Sartre, appears ambivalent on the question of the ultimate function of the novel.

In *One Hundred Years of Solitude* García Márquez provided

his own answer to this question. Rather than efface himself, he made of Macondo and the Buendía family a means of synthesizing his experience without being engulfed by it. In the genealogically linked episodes of this book, persuasive and personable, he blends myth with reality, the improbable with the probable, the timeless and universal with the historical and geographical. He is by turns extravagant and intimate, and avoids the problem of personal responsibility and moral location until the final chapters of the novel. There he introduces himself as a character into the story and uses the work of other modern Latin American novelists as a point of reference. By this and other means he 'opens' his narrative to involve the reader and to make the future of Latin America a direct and urgent issue.[2]

Concern with the responsibility of the Latin American novelist is yet more obvious in the work of Cortázar and José María Arguedas. Though they engaged in bitter polemic about the form this responsibility should take and about the subject matter the novelist should concentrate on, they both had strong feelings on the point of principle. On the face of it the terms of the disagreement between them seem only too familiar. Cortázar is cosmopolitan, a descendant of Borges, and in his turn a glamorous source of influence on younger writers (among them, the Mexican José Agustín, the Chilean Antonio Skarmeta, the Argentinian Manuel Puig and the Puerto Rican Eduardo Díaz Valcarcel;[3] the intellectual to whom cultural relativism is anathema in so far as this means that Latin America is not a full participant in the 'game' and is indulgently assigned a special place in the western tradition; the urban novelist, impatient like Onetti with the 'farce' of pre-Columbian and other 'nativist' fantasies. For him there is nothing inherently sacred about the autochthonous flute which stirs the breast of those in love with ancestral America, as we discover when one of the characters in *Manuel's Book* turns on the gramophone: 'I heard this type of *quena* being recorded in Montparnasse by a Polish Jew, I know the record, I even believe the bloke is called Brinsky, you couldn't get anything more indigenous than him, you agree.' 'Irreverence' towards all myths foisted on his continent is a prerequisite for survival.

At the other pole stands the figure of Arguedas, so much in love with 'our indigenous things' that he cannot write without them;

alive to the inner pulse and the obscure provincial intimacies of Rulfo; suspicious of professionalism and revulsed by the 'stench' of city streets; pained even by the necessity of using Spanish as a literary language. In his novels, the Quechua he learnt as a child expresses the kind of universe dreamed of by the Brazilian Americanists in the first days of Independence; he shows the inner world of people overlooked or misunderstood by generations of socially and politically indignant novelists, even more sensitively than Asturias did that of Gaspar Ilóm. Arguedas could hardly have invested more, or more of himself, in this 'other' America as its martyr.

Yet we perceive powerful coincidences of attitude between these two antagonists. They held friends (Vargas Llosa) and literary comrades (Onetti) in common and publicly acknowledged the objections each made to the other. More striking, each in his own way has ceased to find a 'permanent home' in Latin America, Cortázar by his changed nationality and Arguedas by his suicide. And their novels make it clear that these gestures were not fortuitous or coincidental. The agony of the indigenous Tupac Amaru, contemplated daily by Horacio Oliveira, became the explicit focus of *Manuel's Book,* as the desperate continuation of Latin America's efforts to win a dignified or even an organic independence in this century. After concerning himself with the autonomy of the artist in works like 'The Pursuer' and *Hopscotch,* Cortázar deliberately politicized his prose in *Manuel's Book.* He did this to make people politically aware and to sustain hope in a situation from which, ironically enough, he had withdrawn when he changed his nationality. With Arguedas's *The Fox from Above and the Fox from Below,* so akin to *Manuel's Book* as an open narrative which mixes impersonal narrative with intimate confession, this hope seems to vanish but is sustained, paradoxically, by the author's irreversible passage into silence.

NOTES

Introduction

1 See N. J. Davison, *The concept of Modernism in Hispanic Criticism*, Boulder, Colorado 1966; Octavio Paz, 'El caracol y la sirena (Rubén Darío)', *Cuadrivio*, Mexico 1965; J. N. Nist, *The Modernist Movement in Brazil*, Austin, Texas 1967: and chapters 4 and 5 of my *Latin American Poetry: Origins and Presence*, Cambridge 1975.

2 In *América: novela sin novelistas*, Lima 1933; 2nd edition, expanded and corrected, Santiago 1940.

3 Details of these and other similar works may be found in the bibliography.

4 Quoted in J. M. Cohen's anthology *Writers in the New Cuba*, Harmondsworth 1967, p. 186, which also contains work by most of the writers mentioned below. See also Ernesto Cardenal, *En Cuba*, Buenos Aires 1972, Julio Ortega, *Relato de la Utopía. Notas sobre narrativa cubana de la Revolución*, Barcelona 1973; and Ernesto 'Che' Guevara, *Socialism and Man in Cuba* (London 1968). For Debray see chapter 1.

5 The sections of his revolutionary epic, *El año 59*, published so far, have had a lukewarm reception. See also Carpentier's 'Literatura y conciencia política en América Latina' (1961) and his 'Problemática de la actual novela latinoamericana', both in *Tientos y diferencias*, Mexico 1964.

6 See especially no. 26 (1964) of this review. The thoughts of Vargas Llosa and Cortázar on ceasing to be editors are recorded in no. 67 (1971) and in *Viaje alrededor de una mesa*, Buenos Aires 1970. Although the nature of its financial backing led to its being boycotted by many writers, an important critical rival of *Casa de las Américas*, in the discovery and interpretation of the 'new' Latin American novel, was the Paris-based *Mundo nuevo*, under the editorship of Emir Rodríguez Monegal (1966–8).

7 The bibliography lists general works on the subject, and those dealing, like this one, with particular topics (A. Dorfman 1970; A. Cometti Manzoni 1960; J. Ortega 1968; U. Ospina 1964; J. Sommers 1968; M. C. Suarez Murias 1963; and others). I should emphasize that this study by no means pretends to catalogue every novel of Latin America by period and geographical area, and that its perspective is very much shaped by the modern novelists to whom most attention is paid. In practice this has meant leaving on one side such classic early works as the proto-novel 'guide book' *Lazarillo de ciegos caminantes* (1776) by Alonso Carrió de la Vandera; *El periquillo*

sarniento (1816) by José Joaquín Fernández de Lizardi, a picaresque account of independence struggles in Mexico; *Enriquillo* (1879) by Manuel Jesús de Galván; the *Tradiciones* of Ricardo Palma, with their ironic reflections of life in nineteenth-century Lima; and the historical and nationalist romances of the Uruguayan Eduardo Acevedo Díaz.

1 Settings and people

1 Thomson said of the rivers which gave Europeans access to South America:
   they sweep along,
   And traverse realms unknown and blooming wilds
   And fruitful deserts, worlds of solitude,
   Where the sun smiles and the seasons teem in vain,
   unseen and unenjoy'd

2 Translation of Mrs Horace Mann 1868.

3 The critic Alone (*Don A. Blest Gana. Biografía y crítica*. Santiago 1940, p. 163) is surely wrong to say that Rivas triumphs *over* the upper class; he triumphs within it and adopts its conventions.

4 Further novels by Machado de Assis are listed in the bibliography. D. Woll, in *Machado de Assis: die Entwicklung seiner erzählerischen Werkes* (Braunschweig 1972) gives a good account of Machado de Assis's development as a realist writer.

5 Among them, Jorge Edwards and Juan Agustín Palazuelos.

6 *An Introduction to Spanish-American Literature*, Cambridge 1969, p. 242.

7 Rivera ventured into the jungle as a member of a commission sent out to determine the geographical boundaries of Colombia. There is a striking tribute (1929) to Rivera by the renowned author of 'jungle' stories, Horacio Quiroga, in T. Pérez, ed., *Tres novelas ejemplares*, Havana 1971

8 By Ariel Dorfman in *Imaginación y violencia en América*, Santiago 1970.

9 The various applications of this term have been discussed by Angel Flores, *Hispania* (1955), Luis Leal, *Cuadernos americanos*, CLIII (1967) and critics directly concerned with Carpentier's work (see chapter 3).

10 F. Ellison discusses the novelists of the *sertão* and the sugar plantations nearer the coast in *Brazil's New Novel: Four Northeastern Masters*, Berkeley 1954. They are: José Lins do Rego, Graciliano Ramos, Rachel de Quieroz, and the communist Jorge Amado whose works have been very widely translated.

11 The Spanish troops of the time, however, called the creole rebels of the Independence period 'tupamaros' after their Quechua predecessors, seeing large numbers of Indians in the creole armies of Independence. This is the origin of the name of the guerrillas of modern Uruguay.

12 Another prose work of nineteenth-century Argentina, Lucio Mansilla's *Una excursión a los indios ranqueles* (1870) brings into closer focus what remained 'distant perspectives' in *Facundo*.

13 See A. Cometti Manzoni *El indio en la novela de América*, Buenos Aires 1960; Concha Meléndez, *La novela indianista en Hispanoamérica*, 2nd edition Puerto Rico 1961; D. M. Driver, *The Indian in Brazilian Literature*, New York 1942.

14 In chapter 19 of *El Zarco*, Altamirano enquires into the meaning of the Aztec name of the bandits' hideout, Xochimancas. In quoting historians who refer back to such sixteenth-century sources as Sahagun's *General History of the Things of New Spain* he can be seen beginning to exhume his 'own' heritage through literary scholarship.

15 As he reported in the preface to *Atala*, 1801, Chateaubriand had been inspired to write the epic of natural man in America by the rising of the Natchez against the French in 1727, an event which he had interpreted as an attempt to restore liberty to the New World. As he proceeded with his work his purpose became less political. The profound ambivalences created in him by his conversion to the church and the *ancien régime* later in life, particularly his horror of the half-breed, the aptly-named *bois-brulé*, are well presented by Michel Butor, 'Chateaubriand and Early America', *Inventory* [Repertoires II], New York 1964.

16 See my article (Alcides Arguedas as a "Defender of Indians" in the First and Later Editions of *Raza de bronce*', *Romance Notes*, XIII (1971), pp. 1–7.

17 'El escritor argentino y la tradición', *Discusión*, Buenos Aires 1957.

18 See *El juicio de los parricidas*, Buenos Aires 1956.

2 America's Magic Forest: Miguel Ángel Asturias

1 Quoted by J. E. S. Thompson, *The Rise and Fall of Maya Civilization*, Norman (Oklahoma) 1967.

2 Asturias met Vasconcelos in Mexico where he was Minister of Education in Obregón's government (1920–4) and important in fostering post-revolutionary continental ideals in some respects similar to those of Cuba after 1959. The title of his autobiography, *Ulisés criollo* (1936; *A Mexican Ulysses*, Indiana 1963), intimates his cultural preferences, which by no means involved him in identification with the Indian 'race'.

3 Asturias's translations were published under the titles: *Los dioses, los heroes y los hombres de Guatemala, o el libro del consejo* (Popol vuh), Paris 1927, and *Anales de los Xahil de los indios cakchiqueles de Guatemala*, Guatemala 1937. A. Médiz Bolio's translation of the Chumayel text appeared in 1930, and is the source of the French translation by the Surrealist Benjamin Péret (Paris 1956). A Yucatecan, A. Médiz Bolio was also the author of a Maya revivalist tract *La tierra del faisán y del venado* (1922; 2nd edition with prologues by Alfonso Reyes and E. Abreu Gómez, Mexico 1934), which, like Asturias's legends, draws heavily on Maya literature. Asturias is also editor of *Poesía precolumbina*, Buenos Aires 1960, an anthology of Maya and other American Indian texts. The line numbers mentioned in subsequent references to the *Popol vuh* are those of M. Edmonson's excellent translation, *The Book of Counsel*, New Orleans 1971.

4 Discussing the cycle of Mexican novels about the Tzotzil Maya published in the 1950s and 1960s, Joseph Sommers (*After the Storm. Landmarks of the Modern Mexican Novel*, Albuquerque 1968, p. 169) has emphasized the special achievement of Rosario Castellanos in her novel *Oficio de tinieblas* (1962), also about Maya–*ladino* relationships and also influenced by the *Popol vuh*: 'Catalina Díaz Puilja, the

Tzotzil protagonist, emerges as a genuine literary character, a rarity in the Latin American novel, which almost never succeeds in portraying convincing Indian individuals'.

5 This figure has special connotations in Latin America as a result of José Enrique Rodó's famous essay *Ariel* (Montevideo 1900) whose emphasis is very much on spiritual and aesthetic values.

6 After difficulties under Ubico's dictatorship in Guatemala in the 1930s, Asturias served his country as cultural attaché and ambassador under the revolutionary governments of Arévalo and Arbenz (1945–54), in Mexico and Argentina (his wife is Argentinian). He was deprived of his citizenship between 1954 and 1959.

7 In a letter to Francis de Miomandre, included as a prologue to the *Legends* in most editions.

8 Dorfman argues strongly for its overall unity, and so does R. Callan, *M. A. Asturias* New York 1970, detecting a Jungian substratum in the novel of mythic patterns from Old and New World cultures. The argument was first properly stated by A. Castelpoggi, *M. A. Asturias*, Buenos Aires 1961, who however is prevented from developing it by the basic division of his study into parts named 'Asturias, el poeta narrador' and 'Literatura de tesis' and the placing of *Men of Maize* in the first category. Bellini, *La narrativa di M. A. Asturias*, Milan 1966 was the first to argue convincingly that the novel lacked unity. See also E. Leon Hill, *M.A. Asturias. Lo ancestral en su obra literaria*, New York 1972, who is perhaps too little sceptical of Austurias's populism but offers many perceptive close comments on the novel; and I. Verdugo, *El carácter de la literatura hispanoamericana y la novelística de M. A. Asturias*, Guatemala 1968, pp. 132ff and pp. 193–199.

9 See E. Cardenal, *Homenaje a los indios americanos*, English translation, Johns Hopkins University Press 1972; and S. Clissold, *Latin America, a Cultural Outline*, London 1965, p. 50.

10 See D. W. Foster, *The Myth of Paraguay in the Fiction of Augusto Roa Bastos*, Chapel Hill 1969, who however fails to recognize the influence of classic Guarani texts on Roa Bastos; Arguedas is the subject of chapter 7.

11 I have not seen his last work *Yo el supremo*, an account of Dr Francia's dictatorship.

12 F. Partridge's translation.

13 Asturias began his address to the students of this university on its third anniversary by quoting the hymn he had composed for them: 'Love, work and the idea of the home, the workshop and school are what your name means, oh Fatherland! A home for every man, for every man school, and the workshop for every man.' (Quoted by C. Couffon in his edition of *El problema social del indio*, Paris 1971, p. 133).

3   The genesis of America: Alejo Carpentier

1 A point well made by Claude Dumas, '*El siglo de las luces* de Alejo Carpentier', *Homenaje a Alejo Carpentier*, ed. H. Giacoman, New York 1970, p. 329.

2 i.e. of *The Lost Steps*. Carpentier himself has published musicological studies, notably *La música en Cuba* (1946), Mexico 1956.

3 Included in *Tientos y diferencias*, Mexico 1964. See F. Alegría 'Alejo Carpentier: Realismo Mágico' and Carlos Santander, 'Lo maravilloso en la obra de Alejo Carpentier', both in *Homenaje*.

4 On his travels the hero learns much about Indian America, including the existence of the *Popol vuh*. But even this complex and demanding text is made to fit Carpentier's philosophy, as an intuition of the 'horror' of modern industrialization.

5 The subject of 'The Highroad of St James'.

6 Dumas, p. 357, concurs in this opinion.

7 As the hero of this story goes back in time towards his origins he becomes, like Esteban, a 'wholly sensitive and tactile being', while 'the universe entered his every pore'.

8 For example, Luis Harss in *Into the Mainstream*, New York 1967.

9 Edmundo Desnoes ('El siglo de las luces', *Homenaje*) makes a brilliant implicit comparison between Chateaubriand and Carpentier. See also M. Butor, 'Chateaubriand and Early America'.

10 One of the main consequences of Carpentier's revision of the novel on his return to Cuba in 1959 was a shift of emphasis to Sofía from Esteban, whom she leads in the mass rising against the French, in the appended final paragraphs.

4 Survival in the sullied city: Juan Carlos Onetti

1 Onetti has worked as a professional journalist for most of his life. After the job with Reuters he ran a number of magazines and became an editor of the famous Montevideo newspaper *Marcha*.

2 'Tenía que ser. Y entonces sí que se acabó la patria, se acabó todo'.

3 While deeply read in the contemporary western novel (Proust, Céline, Huxley, Faulkner, Hemingway, Hamsun) he paid attention to only one Latin American predecessor, Roberto Arlt, the novelist of modern Buenos Aires: see Jean Franco, *Introduction to Spanish-American Literature*, p. 304. As the 'first modern novel of Latin America' (Emir Rodríguez Monegal), *No Man's Land* owes much to Arlt's 'anti-literary' style, laconic dialogues and cinematic sequences. Onetti is a fervent admirer of Cortázar's work: see Alvaro Castillo's note on his literary preferences generally in *Homenaje a Onetti*, ed. H. Giacoman, New York 1974.

4 A singer who left his native Toulouse at an early age for the River Plate. His music has been appreciated with such fervour in that part of Latin America that whole books have been devoted to proving that he was born there.

5 Well discussed by Fernando Aínsa, a younger Uruguayan novelist, in *Las trampas de Onetti*, Montevideo 1970; see also Mario Benedetti, 'Juan Carlos Onetti y la aventura del hombre', *Literatura uruguaya del siglo XX*, Montevideo 1963, pp. 76–95.

6 Cf. J. Irby, *La influencia de William Faulkner en cuatro narradores hispanoamericanos*, Mexico 1956.

7 Angel Rama's preface to the 2nd edition of this work is a superb introduction to Onetti's work as a whole: 'Origen de un novelista y de una generación literaria', *El pozo*, Montevideo 1967, pp. 49–100.

8 See Luis Harss, *Into the Mainstream*, p. 200.

5   *Province of dead souls: Juan Rulfo*

1 See J. S. Brushwood, *Mexico in its Novel. A Nation's Search for Identity*, Austin 1966, p. 33.
2 A native of the province of Jalisco, to the north west of Mexico City, Rulfo witnessed as a child both the loss of his family's estates to the Revolution and the violence of the *cristero* counter-attacks, which were especially brutal in that part of Mexico. Even after coming to the capital, where he has for long been employed in the National Indigenist Institute, he has retained strong links with rural Mexico. See his *Autobiografía armada*, Buenos Aires 1973.
3 This novel was awarded an important literary prize in Mexico, and was edited with illustrations by Diego Rivera, which make remarkable use of the literary conventions of the screenfold painted books of ancient Mexico.
4 *After the Storm*, p. 88. This study contains an excellent comparison of Rulfo's writing with that of Agustín Yáñez (see below).
5 A point well made by Jean Franco in *The Modern Culture of Latin America: Society and the Artist*, London 1967, pp. 169–170.
6 English translation in J. M. Cohen's *Latin American Writing Today*, Harmondsworth 1967.
7 In *The Plumed Serpent, The Power and the Glory, Les Tarahumaras* and *Under the Volcano*, respectively.
8 Azuela is also the author of the useful historical survey *Cien años de la novela mexicana*, Mexico 1947, which includes novels prior to his own.
9 See Paz's prologue to Fuentes's *Cuerpos y ofrendas*, Mexico 1972, which refers ungenerously to Rulfo's provincialism.
10 Mexico 1952; subsequently published as a full 'scientific' study as *Chamula. Un pueblo indio de los altos de Chiapas*, Mexico 1959.

6   *Intellectual geography: Julio Cortázar*

1 *La isla a mediodía y cuentos*, Barcelona 1971, is a recent collection of Cortázar's short stories. The story by him on which Antonioni based his film 'Blow-Up' is not this one but 'Las babas del diablo'.
2 The words of the title are both anagrams of *poemas* (poems).
3 Sharon Spencer devotes pp. 203–9 of her *Space, Time and Structure in the Modern Novel*, New York 1971, to *Hopscotch*.
4 This was the opinion of the reviewer of *Hopscotch* in the *TLS* (1967); 'if. . .the endless "intellectual" exchanges of Oliveira and his friends are meant to convey that Western dialectics are inconsequential, Señor Cortázar must produce far more authentic dialectics than these. The force of his case against dialectical apprehension lies in Oliveira's antics, not in his rather fake-oriental pronouncements.'
5 Excellently analysed by D. Musselwhite ('"El perseguidor" un modelo para desarmar', *Nuevos aires*, 8, 1972) as a turning point in Cortázar's work.
6 See *La casilla de los Morelli*, edited by Julio Ortega, Barcelona 1973, a compendium of Morelliana.
7 Cortázar has lived in Europe since 1951, and was born there (in Brussels) of parents of Argentine nationality but of French, German and Basque extraction. As a young man he had an academic post in

Mendoza, which he resigned sooner than have Perón terminate it for him.

7 Tupac Amaru dismembered: José María Arguedas

1 Arguedas shot himself in a room in the National Agrarian University in Peru in 1969, leaving this novel to be published posthumously. The previous suicide attempt had come after a nervous breakdown 1943–4.
2 In *Life*, 7 April 1969.
3 Vargas Llosa is, for example, author of an important prologue to the Cuban edition of *Los ríos profundos*, 1965: 'Ensoñación y magia en José María Arguedas'.
4 With the help of H. Trimborn's German version, *Zauber und Dämonen in Inkareich*, Berlin 1939–41.
5 One of his last publications was a 'Third World' manifesto on the Vietnam War: 'Quollan, Vietnam llaqtaman' included in C. Lévano's *Arguedas: Un sentimiento trágico de la vida*, Lima 1969).
6 In his *Siete ensayos de interpretación de la realidad peruana*, Lima 1928.
7 There is however an interesting continuity between Alegría's *La serpiente de oro*, 1935, in which the mountain river Marañón is seen as a serpent (*amaru*) and a source of strength, and Arguedas's writing.
8 See his 'Los mitos quechuas posthispánicos', *Casa de las Américas* 47 (1968), pp. 17–29. Other studies include: *Mitos, leyendas y cuentos peruanos*, Lima 1947: *Canciones y cuentos del pueblo quechua*, Lima 1949; and *Cuentos mágico-realistas y canciones de fiestas tradicionales en el valle de Mantaro*, Lima 1953.
9 Recently edited by W. Rowe, Oxford 1973; Rowe provides an extremely acute introduction to Arguedas's work in general in this edition, on which I have drawn here.
10 See, for example, J. P. L. Baudin, *L'Empire socialiste des Inka*, Paris 1928, and the incisive modern scholarship of John V. Murra, in 'The Economic Organization of the Inca State', unpublished Ph.D. diss. University of Chicago 1956.
11 A searching (and unindulgent) critique of Arguedas and his work is made by E. Gerhards, *Das Bild des Indio in der peruanischen Literatur: Mythos und Mystifikation der indianischen Welt bei J. M. Arguedas*, Berlin 1972.
12 Published in the original in *Campesino* (Lima) 2 (August 1969), and again in *Amaru*, no. 11. Arguedas's residual optimism has been justified to some extent since his death: Quechua, for example, is now recognized as an official language of Peru.

8 Social structures: Mario Vargas Llosa

1 Quoted by J. M. Oviedo, *Mario Vargas Llosa: La invención de una realidad*, Barcelona 1970, p. 99.
2 Oviedo, p. 108.
3 Where he became a student at San Marcos, the university at which Arguedas taught. He then went to Paris, like Cortázar and García Márquez, and later studied for a doctorate at the University of Madrid. He began to win recognition as a writer with the award of the

Leopoldo Alas prize for *Los jefes*, 1958, and the Biblioteca breve prize offered by the Barcelona publishing house Seix Barral, for *La ciudad y los perros* in 1962. For his remarks on Arguedas and on the Indianist novel, see his 'José María Arguedas y el indio', published as the prologue to *Los ríos profundos*, Havana 1965.

4 See his *Historia secreta de una novela*, Barcelona 1971.

5 In *El combate imaginario; las cartas de batalla de Joanot Martorell* (with Martin de Riquer), Barcelona 1972.

6 The epigraph of *Conversation in The Cathedral* is from Balzac's *Petites misères de la vie conjugale:* 'Il faut avoir fouillé toute la vie sociale pour être un vrai romancier, vu que le roman est l'histoire privée des nations'.

7 'The Latin American Novel Today', *Books Abroad* 44 (1970), p. 15. See also his 'Fate and Mission of the Writer in Latin America' (his speech on being awarded the Rómulo Gallegos prize in Caracas in 1967), *Haravec* (Lima), 4 (1967), pp. 56–9.

9 An end to secular solitude: Gabriel García Márquez

1 At one point José Arcadio discovers (erroneously) that Macondo is surrounded by water on all sides, precisely the situation of Aztlan, the tribal home of the Aztecs which, no doubt for similar psychological reasons, became the mythical Eden of the Chicanos and other Spanish-Americans subjected more directly to the power of the U.S.

2 'Sólo un personaje permanence inmovil y vidente, en el centro de todo, como auténtico tronco secular de la familia: Úrsula Iguarán es ese principio ordenador en medio del caos de los tiempos, la razón doméstica en medio del infinito peregrinaje de los hijos que desparraman el apellido Buendía igual que una semilla en el viento'. J. M. Oviedo, 'Macondo: un territorio mágico y americano', *Nueve asedios a García Márquez*, M. Benedetti *et al.*, Santiago 1969, p. 95.

3 Like him, she takes part in conversations with ghosts.

4 'Los resabios faulknerianos han desaparecido; "los combatí leyendo a Hemingway", bromea García Márquez'. M. Vargas Llosa, 'García Márquez: de Aracataca a Macondo', *Nueve asedios*, p. 137.

5 Angel Rama, 'Un novelista de la violencia americana', *Nueve asedios*, p. 115.

6 See Carlos Blanco Aguinaga, 'Sobre la lluvia y la historia en las ficciones de García Márquez', *Narradores hispanoamericanos de hoy*, ed. J. B. Avalle-Arce, Chapel Hill 1973, p. 55–72.

7 Umberto Eco, *Opera aperta*, Milan 1967 (2nd edition).

8 This reading is confirmed by García Márquez's more recent novel *The Autumn of the Patriarch* (*El otóno del patriarca*, 1975) which is discussed briefly in note 2 to chapter 10.

10 A permanent home?

1 Mario Vargas Llosa, *Historia de un deicidio*, Barcelona 1971.

2 García Márquez's political anxieties are made quite explicit in his subsequent novel *The Autumn of the Patriarch*, which provides the same sort of sequel to *One Hundred Years of Solitude* as Cortázar's *Manuel's Book* does to *Hopscotch*. The 'patriarch' shows many family

likenesses with the Buendías, though very little of their charm.
Moreover, though the place he rules over resembles Macondo in its
provinciality and in many of its oddities, it is a capital city, and
therefore directly and continuously vulnerable to the foreign powers
which have exploited Latin America since its supposed 'Independence',
the most voracious and sophisticated being the U.S.A. The novel
(which I read after writing this book) is too complex to deal with at all
adequately here. If anything, it is an even more 'Latin American'
novel than *One Hundred Years*, and draws to great advantage on the
literary traditions of the sub-continent. The 'Caribbean' Carpentier,
for example, is alluded to even more tellingly. In the patriarch himself
we find traits of Rulfo's Pedro Páramo and Fuentes's Artemio Cruz
alike. While abject and absurd to the outside world, this figure is
all-powerful in his own place, which is said to be both a risible 'nigger
whore-house' and a 'nightmare realm' like the jungle in J. E. Rivera's
The Vortex. As a classic Latin American dictator he specifically recalls
Vargas Llosa's Odría, Reinaldo Arenas's Iturbide, and the 'president'
of Miguel Ángel Asturias. Indeed, García Márquez uses this last, the
Guatemalan Estrada Cabrera, to take still further the whole matter
of the function of literature in Latin America. We are shown the
Modernist poet Rubén Darío, who in history was Estrada Cabrera's
honoured guest, exciting the patriarch with' the revelation of written
beauty'. Against this illusory power, García Márquez again subtly
invokes the support of his contemporaries, above all Cortázar, with
his agonized concern with the birthright of the Latin American child
(E)Manuel. But his exasperated conclusion, at least in this novel,
is that in his present situation the Latin American writer can be no
more than an ineffectual 'poor dreamer'.

3 See, respectively, *Inventando que sueño*, Mexico 1968; *Desnudo en
el tejado*, Havana 1969; *La traición de Rita Hayworth*, Buenos Aires
1969; *Figuraciones en el mes de marzo*, Barcelona 1972. In Agustín's
novel (H. Oliveira appears in person, to combat the police and the
Gekreptens of Mexico City.

SELECT BIBLIOGRAPHY

1 General

Adams, M. I., *Three Authors of Alienation* [María Lusia Bombal, Onetti Carpentier], Austin 1975

Alegría, F., *Historia de la novela hispanoamericana*, Mexico 1966 (3rd edition)

– *Literatura y revolución*, Mexico 1971

Amorós, A., *Introducción a la novela hispanoamericana actual*, Madrid 1971

Auerbach, E., *Mimesis. The Representation of Reality in Western Literature*, New York 1957

Avalle-Acre, J. B. (ed.), *Narradores hispanoamericanos de hoy*, Simposio, Chapel Hill 1973

Azuela, M., *Cien años de novela mexicana*, Mexico 1947

Benedetti, M., *Letras del continente mestizo*, Montevideo 1967

Brotherston, G. and M. Vargas Llosa (eds.), *Seven Stories from Spanish America*, Oxford 1968

Brushwood, J. S., *Mexico in its Novel. A Nation's Search for Identity*, Austin 1966

Carpentier, A., 'Literatura y conciencia política en América Latina' (and other essays), *Tientos y diferencias*, Mexico 1964

Cohen, J. M. (ed.), *Latin American Writing Today*, Harmondsworth 1967

– *Writers in the New Cuba*, Harmondsworth 1967

Cometti Manzoni, A., *El indio en la novela de América*, Buenos Aires 1960

Conte, R., *Lenguaje y violencia: introducción a la nueva novela hispanoamericana*, Madrid 1972

Coulthard, G. R., *Race and Colour in Caribbean Literature*, Oxford 1962

Cruz, S. de la, *Nuevos novelistas*, Mexico 1955

Debray, R., *Revolution in the Revolution?*, Harmondsworth 1967

Donoso, J., *Historia personal del 'boom'*, Barcelona 1973

Dorfman, A., *Imaginación y violencia en América*, Santiago 1970

Driver, D. M., *The Indian in Brazilian Literature*, New York 1942

Eco, U., *Opera aperta*, Milan 1967 (2nd edition)

Ellison, F., *Brazil's New Novel: Four Northeastern Masters*, Berkeley 1954

Flores, A. and R. Silva Cáceres, (eds.), *La novela hispanoamericana actual*, New York 1971 (a collection of essays)

Franco, J., *The Modern Culture of Latin America: Society and the Artist*, London 1967

– *An Introduction to Spanish-American Literature*, Cambridge 1969

Fuentes, Carlos, *La nueva novela hispanoamericana*, Mexico 1969

Gallagher, D. P., *Modern Latin American Literature*, OUP 1973 (chapters on García Márquez, Vargas Llosa, Cabrera Infante)

Gertel, Z., *La novela hispanoamericana contemporánea*, Buenos Aires 1970

Gonzalez Bermejo, E., *Cosas de escritores* (García Márquez, Vargas Llosa, Cortázar), Montevideo 1971

González del Valle, L. and V. Cabrera, *La nueva ficción hispanoamericana a través de Miguel Ángel Asturias y Gabriel García Márquez*, New York 1972

Guevara, Ernesto 'Che', *Obra revolucionaria*, prologue and selection by Roberto Fernández Retamar, Mexico 1967

– *Socialism and Man in Cuba, and other works*, London 1968

Harss, L., *Into the Mainstream*, New York 1967. In Spanish as: *Los nuestros*, Buenos Aires 1966

Irby, J., *La influencia de William Faulkner en cuatro narradores* (Lino Novas Calvo, Onetti, Revueltas and Rulfo), Mexico 1956

Jones, C. A., *Three Spanish American Novelists Gallegos, Fuentes, Icaza: A European View*, London 1967

Lafforgue, J. (ed.), *Nueva novela latinoamericana*. 2 volumes, 1969 and 1972

Langford, W. M., *The Mexican Novel comes of Age*, Notre Dame 1971

Lazo, R., *La novela andina. Pasado y futuro*, Mexico 1971

Lichtblau, M. I., *The Argentine Novel in the 19th Century*, New York 1959,

Loveluck, J., *La novela hispanoamericana*, Santiago 1966 (2nd edition)

Lukács, G., *Studies in European Realism*, New York 1964

– *The Theory of the Novel*, Cambridge, Mass., 1971

Meléndez, C., *La novela indianista en Hispanoamerica*, Puerto Rico 1961 (2nd edition)

Ocampo de Gomez, A. M., *Novelistas iberoamericanos contemporáneos. Obras y bibliografía crítica*, Mexico 1971–

Ortega, J., *La contemplación y la fiesta*, Lima 1968

– *Relato de la Utopía. Notas sobre narrativa cubana de la Revolución*, Barcelona 1973

Ospina, U., *Problemas y perspectivas de la novela américana*, Bogotá 1964

Pérez, Trinidad (ed.), *Tres novelas ejemplares* [*La vorágine; Doña Bárbara* and *Don Segundo Sombra*]; Recopilación de textos, Havana 1971

Prieto, A., *Sociología del público argentino*, Buenos Aires 1956

– *La literatura autobiográfica argentina*, Buenos Aires 1962

Rodríguez Monegal, E., *Narradores de esta América*, Montevideo 1969 (2nd edition)

– *El arte de narrar*, Montevideo 1969

Sánchez, L. A., *América: novela sin novelistas*, Lima 1933; Santiago 1940 (2nd edition)

– *Proceso y contenido de la novela hispanoamericana*, Madrid 1953

Sartre, J. P., *Qu'est-ce que la littérature*, Paris 1948

Schulman, I. (with M. P. González, J. Loveluck and F. Alegría), *Coloquios sobre la novela hispanoamericana*, Mexico 1967

Sommers, J., *After the Storm. Landmarks of the Modern Mexican Novel*, Albuquerque 1968

Spell, J. R., *Contemporary Spanish American Fiction*, Chapel Hill 1944 (reprinted New York 1968)

Spencer, Sharon, *Space, Time and Structure in the Modern Novel*, New York 1971

Suarez Murias, M. C., *La novela romántica en Hispanoamerica*, New York 1963

Torres Rioseco, A., *Grandes novelistas de la América hispana: i Los novelistas de la tierra*, Berkeley and Los Angeles 1941; II *Los novelistas de la ciudad*, Berkeley and Los Angeles 1943 (both in one volume 1949)

Uslar Pietri, R., *Breve historia de la novela hispanoamericana*, Caracas 1966

Valenzuela, V. M., *Contemporary Latin American Writers*, New York 1971

Vargas Llosa, M., 'The Latin American Novel Today', *Books Abroad*, 44 (1970)

Vázquez Amaral, J., *The Contemporary Latin American Narrative*, New York 1971

Watt, I., *The Rise of the Novel*, Berkeley 1962

Yáñez, A., *El contexto social de la literatura iberoamericana*, Acapulco 1967

Zum Felde, A. de, *La narrativa en Hispanoamerica*, Madrid 1964

See also the following periodical publications: *Books Abroad* now *World Literature Today* (Norman); *Casa de las Américas* (Havana); *Mundo nuevo* (Paris), 1966–8; *Nueva narrativa hispanoamericana*, 1971–; *Review* (New York)

2 Works by and on the principal Latin American authors mentioned in the text

Alegría, Ciro
- 1935 *La serpiente de oro*, Santiago. *The Golden Serpent*, tr. Harriet de Onis, New York 1963
- 1941 *El mundo es ancho y ajeno*, Lima. *Broad and Alien is the World*, tr. Harriet de Onis, New York

Alencar, Jose Martiniano de
- 1857 *O Guarani*, Rio
- 1866 *Iracema*, Rio. *Iracema, the Honey-Lips*, tr. I. Burton, London 1886
- 1874 *Ubirajara. Lenda tupi*, Rio

Altamirano, Ignacio Manuel
- 1901 *El Zarco. Episodio de la vida mexicana en 1861–3*, Barcelona
- Martínez, J. L. (ed.), *La literatura nacional*, Mexico 1949
- Warner, R. E., *Bibliografía de I. M. Altamirano*, Mexico 1955

Amado, Jorge
- 1942 *Terras do sem-fim*, São Paulo. *The Violent Land*, tr. Samuel Putnam, New York 1965

Arenas, Reinaldo
- 1967 *El mundo alucinante*, Mexico. *Hallucinations, being an account of the life and adventures of Friar Servando Teresa de Meir*, tr. G. Brotherston, London 1971

Arguedas, Alcides
- 1919 *Raza de bronce*, La Paz
- Medinaceli, C., *La inactualidad de Alcides Arguedas*, La Paz 1972

Arguedas, José María
- 1935 *Agua*, Lima
- 1938 *Canto Kechwa*, Lima
- 1941 *Yawar fiesta*, Lima. Revised edition 1958. (*Yawar* is the Quechua for 'blood')
- 1954 *Diamantes y pedernales*, Lima. Short stories. *Diamonds and flints*
- 1958 *Los ríos profundos*, Buenos Aires. Havana 1965, with a prologue by Mario Vargas Llosa, 'Ensoñación y magia en José María Arguedas'. *The deep rivers*. Ed. W. Rowe, Oxford 1973

- 1961 *El sexto*, Lima. (The name of a gaol)

Arguedas, José María
- 1962 *Tupac Amaru Kamaq Taytanchisman. Haylli-Taki. A nuestro padre creador Tupac Amaru. Himno-cancion*, Lima
- 1964 *Todas las sangres*, Buenos Aires. *Every Blood*
- 1967 *Amor mundo y todos los cuentos de José María Arguedas*, Lima. Collected short stories
- 1971 *El zorro de arriba y el zorro de abajo*, Buenos Aires. *The fox from above and the fox from below*
- Gerhards, E., *Das Bild des Indio in der peruanischen Literatur: Mythos und Mystifikation der indianischen Welt bei J. M. Arguedas*, Berlin 1972
- Lévano, C., *Arguedas: un sentimiento trágico de la vida* Lima 1969
- Marín, Gladys S. C., *La experiencia americana de José María Arguedas*, Buenos Aires 1973

Arlt, Roberto
- 1926 *El juguete rabioso*, Buenos Aires
- 1929 *Los siete locos*, Buenos Aires
- 1931 *Los Lanzallamas*, Buenos Aires
- *Novelas completas y cuentos*, Buenos Aires 1963. 3 vols.
- Núñez, A., *La obra narrativa de Roberto Arlt*, Buenos Aires 1968

Asturias, Miguel Ángel
- 1923 *El problema social del indio*, Guatemala. Ed., with other texts, 1926–1927, by C. Couffon, Paris 1971
- 1930 *Leyendas de Guatemala*, Madrid. *Legends of Guatemala*
- 1946 *El señor presidente*, Mexico. Buenos Aires 1948. *The President*, tr. F. Partridge, London 1963
- 1949 *Hombres de maíz*, Buenos Aires. *Men of Maize*
- 1950 *Viento fuerte*, Buenos Aires. *The Cyclone*, tr. D. Flakoll and Claribel Alegría, London 1967; *Strong Wind*, tr. G. Rabassa, New York 1968
- 1954 *El papa verde*, Buenos Aires. *The Green Pope*, tr. G. Rabassa, London 1971
- 1956 *Week-end en Guatemala*, Buenos Aires
- 1960 *Los ojos de los enterrados*, Buenos Aires. *The Eyes of the Buried*
- 1961 *El alhajadito*, Buenos Aires. *The Bejewelled Boy*, tr. M. Shuttleworth, New York 1971
- 1963 *Mulata de tal*, Buenos Aires. *The Mulatta and Mr Fly*, tr. G. Rabassa, London 1967
- 1964 *Teatro*, Buenos Aires. Collected plays
- 1965 *Clarivigilia primeraveral*, Buenos Aires. Poem. *Spring Vigil*
- 1969 *Maladrón. Epopeya de los Andes verdes*, Buenos Aires
- 1970 *Latinoamerica y otros ensayos*, Madrid
- 1971 *Torotumbo*, Barcelona
- 1971 *Trois des quatre soleils*, tr. C. Couffon, Geneva. *Three of the Four Suns*
- 1971 *Novelas y cuentos de juventud*, Paris. Early fiction
- 1972 *Viernes de dolores*, Buenos Aires
- 1973 *Lo mejor de mi obra. Autoantología*, Barcelona
- Andrea, P. F. de, *M. A. Asturias; anticipo bibliográfico* Mexico 1969
- Bellini, G., *La narrativa di M. A. Asturias*, Milan 1966. Spanish translation, Buenos Aires 1969
- Callan, R., *M. A. Asturias*, New York 1970
- Castelpoggi, A., *M. A. Asturias*, Buenos Aires 1961

- Giacoman, H. (ed.), *Homenaje a Asturias,* New York 1971
- Leon Hill, Eladia, *M. A. Asturias. Lo ancestral en su obra literaria,* New York 1972
- Menton, S., *Historia crítica de la novela guatemalteca,* Guatemala 1960
- Pilon, Marta, *M. A. Asturias. Semblanza para el estudio de su vida y obra con una selección de poemas y prosas,* Guatemala 1968
- Verdugo, I., *El carácter de la literatura hispanoamericana y la novelística de M. A. Asturias,* Guatemala 1968
Azuela, Mariano
- 1915 *Los de abajo. Novela de la revolucion mexicana,* El Paso, Mexico 1925. *The Underdogs,* tr. E. Munguia, London 1930
- 1917 *Las moscas,* Mexico
- 1918 *Los caciques,* Mexico. This and *Las moscas* tr. L. B. Simpson *Two novels of Mexico: The Flies and The Bosses,* Berkeley 1956
Barrios, Eduardo
- 1950 *Los hombres del hombre,* Santiago. *The Men of the Man*
Benedetti, Mario
- 1960 *La tregua,* Montevideo. *The Truce,* tr. B. Graham, New York 1969
- 1965 *Gracias por el fuego,* Montevideo. *Thanks for the light*
Blest Gana, Alberto
- 1862 *Martín Rivas,* Santiago
- 1897 *Durante la Reconquista,* Santiago
- Alone [Díaz Arrieta, Hernan] *Don A. Blest Gana. Biografía y crítica,* Santiago 1940
- Latcham, Richard, *Blest Gana y la novela realista,* Santiago 1959
Borges, Jorge Luis
- 1944 *Ficciones,* Buenos Aires. *Fictions,* tr. A. Kerrigan, New York 1962
- 1949 *El aleph,* Buenos Aires
- Becco, H. J., *J. L. Borges. Bibliografía total,* Buenos Aires 1974
- Brotherston, G. and P. Hulme (eds.), *J. L. Borges, Ficciones,* London 1976
Cabrera Infante, Guillermo
- 1967 *Tres tristes tigres,* Barcelona. *Three Trapped Tigers,* tr. D. Gardiner and S. J. Levine, New York 1971
Cambaceres, Eugenio
- 1885 *Sin rumbo,* Buenos Aires. *Drifting*
Carpentier, Alejo
- 1933 *Ecue-yamba-O,* Buenos Aires 1967 (2nd edition)
- 1949 *El reino de este mundo,* Mexico. *The Kingdom of this World,* tr. H. de Onis, New York 1957
- 1953 *Los pasos perdidos,* Mexico. *The Lost Steps,* tr. H. de Onis, New York 1957
- 1956 *El acoso,* Buenos Aires. 'Manhunt', tr. H. de Onis, Noon, III (1959)
- 1958 *Guerra del tiempo. Tres relatos y una novela*: 'El acoso', 'El camino de Santiago', 'El derecho de asilo' and 'Viaje a la semilla, Mexico. *War of time,* tr. F. Partridge, New York 1970 (Includes: 'Manhunt', 'The Highroad of St James', 'Right of Sanctuary', 'Journey back to the Source' and two other stories, 'Like the Night' ('Semejante a la noche') and 'The Chosen' ('Los fugitivos')
- 1962 *El siglo de las luces,* Havana, *Explosion in a Cathedral,* tr. J. Sturrock, London 1963
- 1964 *Tientos y diferencias,* Mexico. Essays
  1974 *Recurso del metodo,* Mexico

Carpentier Alejo
  – Giacoman, H. (ed.), *Homenaje a Alejo Carpentier*, New York 1970
  – Márquez Rodríguez, A., *La obra narrativa de A. Carpentier*, Caracas 1970
  – Palermo. Z. et al., *Historia y mito en la obra de Carpentier*, Buenos Aires 1972
Castellanos, Rosario
  – 1957 *Balún Canaán*, Mexico. *The Nine Guardians*, tr. Irene Nicholson, London 1959
  – 1962 *Oficio de tinieblas*, Mexico. *Office of darkness*
Cortázar, Julio
  – 1949 *Los reyes*, Buenos Aires *The Kings*
  – 1951 *Bestiario*, Buenos Aires. *Bestiary*. Short stories
  – 1956 *Final del juego*, Mexico. Expanded edition Buenos Aires 1964. Short stories. *End of the Game*, tr. P. Blackburn, London 1968 (includes stories from *Bestiary* and *The secret weapons*)
  – 1959 *Las armas secretas*, Buenos Aires. *The secret weapons*. Short stories
  – 1960 *Los premios*, Buenos Aires. *The Winners*, tr. E. Kerrigan, New York 1965
  – 1962 *Historias de cronopios y famas*, Buenos Aires. *Cronopios and Famas*, tr. P. Blackburn, New York 1969
  – 1963 *Rayuela*, Buenos Aires. *Hopscotch*, tr. G. Rabassa, London 1967
  – 1966 *Todos los fuegos el fuego*, Buenos Aires. *All the fires the fire*. Short stories
  – 1967 *La vuelta al día en ochenta mundos*, Mexico. *Round the day in eighty worlds*
  – 1968 *62. Modelo para armas*, Buenos Aires. *62. Model kit*, tr. G. Rabassa, London 1976
  – 1970 *Último round*, Mexico. *Last round*
  – 1971 *Pameos y meopas*, Barcelona. Poems
  – 1971 *La isla a mediodía y otros cuentos*, Madrid. Collected short stories
  – 1973 *Libro de Manuel*, Buenos Aires. *Manuel's book*
  – 1974 *Octaedro*, Madrid. Short stories
  – Curutchet, J. C., *J. Cortázar o la crítica de la razón pragmática*, Madrid 1972
  – Garfield, Evelyn P., *Julio Cortázar*, New York 1975
  – Giacoman, H. (ed.), *Homenaje a J. Cortázar*, New York 1972
  – Jitrik, N. et al., *La vuelta a Cortázar en nueve ensayos*, Buenos Aires 1969
  – Roy, J., *J. Cortázar ante su sociedad*, Barcelona 1974
  – Sosnowski, S., *J. Cortázar; una búsqueda mítica*, Buenos Aires 1973
Cunha, Euclides da
  – 1902 *Os sertões. Campanha de Canudos*, Rio. *Rebellion in the Backlands* tr. Samuel Putnam, Chicago 1944
  – Andrade, O. de Souza, *Historia e interpretacão de Os Sertões*, São Paulo 1966 (3rd edition)
Desnoes, Edmundo
  – 1965 *El cataclismo*, Havana
  – 1967 *Memorias del subdesarrollo*, Havana. *Inconsolable Memories*, tr. the author, New York 1967. Later editions, and the film of the book, as *Memories of Underdevelopment*
Donoso, José
  – 1957 *Coronación*, Santiago. *Coronation*, tr. Jocasta Goodwin, London 1965

– 1965 *Este domingo*, Santiago, *This Sunday*, tr. Lorraine O'Grady Freeman, London 1968
– 1970 *El obsceno pájaro de la noche*, Barcelona 1970. *The Obscene Bird of Night*, tr. Hardie St Martin and L. Mades, New York 1973
– 1973 *Tres novelitas burguesas*, Barcelona. *Three bourgeois novelettes*

Edwards, Jorge
– 1967 *Las máscaras*, Barcelona. *The masks*
– 1971 *El peso de la noche*, Barcelona. *The weight of the night*

Fuentes Carlos,
– 1954 *Los días enmascarados*, Mexico. *The masked days*
– 1958 *La región más transparente*, Mexico. *Where the Air is Clear*, tr. S. Hileman, New York 1960
– 1959 *Las buenas consciencias*, Mexico. *The Good Conscience*. New York 1971
– 1962 *La muerte de Artemio Cruz*, Mexico. *The Death of Artemio Cruz*, tr. S. Hileman, London 1964
– 1962 *Aura*, Mexico
– 1967 *Cambio de piel*, Mexico. *Change of Skin*, tr. S. Hileman, New York 1968
– 1969 *Cumpleaños*, Mexico. *Birthday*
– 1972; *Cuerpos y ofrendas*, Mexico (includes *Aura*, *Cumpleaños* and other novellas and short stories)
– Giacoman, H. (ed.), *Homenaje a Carlos Fuentes*, New York 1971
– Guzmán, D. de, *Carlos Fuentes*, New York 1972

Gallegos, Rómulo
– 1929 *Doña Bárbara*, Caracas. Tr. R. Malloy, London 1931
– Bellini, G., *Il romanzo di R. Gallegos*, Milan 1962
– Dunham, L., *R. Gallegos, vida y obra*, Mexico 1957
– Ulrich, L., *R. Gallegos. Estudio sobre el arte de narrar*, Caracas 1967

García Márquez, Gabriel
– 1955 *La hojarasca*, Bogotá. *Leaf storm and other stories*, tr. G. Rabassa, London 1972
– 1961 *El coronel no tiene quien le escriba*, Medellín; Mexico 1963 *No one Writes to the Colonel*, tr. J. S. Bernstein, London 1971
– 1961 *La mala hora*, Madrid; Mexico 1966 – the first edition recognized by the author. *The Evil Hour*
– 1962 *Los funerales de la Mamá Grande*, Mexico. *Big Mama's Funeral*, in *No one Writes to the Colonel*. Short stories.
– 1967 *Cien años de soledad*, Buenos Aires. *One Hundred Years of Solitude*, tr. G. Rabassa, New York 1970
– 1970 *Relatos de un náufrago*, Barcelona. *Tales of a shipwrecked man*
– 1972 *La increíble y triste historia de la cándida Erendia y de su abuela desalmada*, Barcelona. 7 short stories
– 1972 *El negro que hizo esperar a los ángeles*, Montevideo. Novella
– 1974 *Ojos de perro azul*, Esplugas de Llobregat. Collected short stories
– 1974 *Cuando era felz e indocumentado*, Esplugas de Llobregat. Newspaper articles
– 1975 *El otoño del patriarca*, Barcelona. *The Autumn of the Patriarch*, tr. G. Rabassa, London 1975
– Arnau, C., *El mundo mítico de G. G. M.*, Barcelona 1972
– Benedetti, M. *et al.*, *Nueve asedios a García Márquez*, Santiago 1969

-- Bolletino, V., *Breve estudio de la novelística de García Márquez*, Madrid 1973
- Fernandez-Braso, M., *La soledad de G.G.M.*, Barcelona 1972
- Gullón, R., *García Márquez o el olvidado arte de contar*, Madrid 1970
- Martínez, P. S., *Recopilación de textos sobre G.G.M.*, Havana 1969
- Vargas Llosa, M., *Historia de un deicidio*, Barcelona 1971

Güiraldes, Ricardo
- 1926 *Don Segundo Sombra*, Buenos Aires. *Don Segundo Sombra, Shadows on the Pampas*, tr. H. de Onis, introduction by Waldo Frank, London 1935. Ed. R. Beardsell, Oxford 1972
- Ghiano, J. C., *Ricardo Güiraldes*, Buenos Aires 1966
- Previtale, G., *R. Güiraldes and Don Segundo Sombra*, New York 1963

Icaza, Jorge
- 1934 *Huasipungo*, Quito. Tr. M. Savill, London 1962. *Huasipungo. The Villagers*, tr. B. M. Dudley, Carbondale 1964 ('from the expanded version of 1951').
- García, A., *Sociología de la novela indigenista en el Ecuador*, Quito 1969
- Sacoto, A., *The Indian in the Ecuadorian Novel*, New York 1967

Isaacs, Jorge
- 1867 *María, Novela americana*, Bogotá. *María, a South American Romance*, tr. T. A. Janvier, New York 1925
- McGrady, D., *Jorge Isaacs*, New York 1972

Lezama Lima, José
- 1966 *Paradiso*, Havana. Tr. G. Rabassa, New York 1974

López y Fuentes, Gregorio
- 1932 *La tierra*, Mexico. Ed. H. A. Holmes Boston 1949
- 1935 *El indio*, Mexico. Tr. Anita Brenner, New York 1937 (English edition as *They that Reap*)

Machado de Assis, Joaquim Maria
- 1880 *Memorias posthumas de Bras Cubas*, Rio. *Epitaph of a Small Winner*, tr. W. L. Grossman, New York 1952
- 1892 *Quincas Borba*, Rio. *Philosopher or Dog?*, tr. Cotilde Wilson, New York 1954 (English version as *The Heritage of Quincas Borba*)
- 1900 *Dom Casmurro*, Rio. Tr. Helen Caldwell, with an introduction by Waldo Frank, New York 1953
- 1904 *Esau e Jacob*, Rio. *Esau and Jacob*, tr. Helen Caldwell, London 1966
- 1908 *Memorial de Ayres*, Rio. *Consellor Ayres' Memorial*, tr. Helen Caldwell, Berkeley 1972
- Caldwell, H., *Machado de Assis; the Brazilian Master and his Novels*, Berkeley 1970
- Caldwell, H., *The Brazilian Othello of Machado de Assis. A Study of Dom Casmurro*, Berkeley 1960
- Castello, J. A., *Realidade e ilusão em Machado de Assis*, São Paulo 1969
- Pacheco, J., *O realismo*, São Paulo 1968
- Woll, D., *Machado de Assis; die Entwicklung seiner erzählerischen Werkes*, Braunschweig 1972

Mallea, Eduardo
- 1930 *La bahía del silencio*, Buenos Aires. *The Bay of Silence*, tr. E. Grummon, New York 1944
- 1938 *Fiesta en noviembre*, Buenos Aires. *Fiesta in November*, tr. A. de Solá, London 1969

- 1941 *Todo verdor perecerá*, Buenos Aires. *All Green Shall Perish*, tr. J. B. Hughes, London 1967; *Chaves and other stories*, London 1970
- Lichtblau, M. I., *El arte estilístico de E. Mallea*, Buenos Aires 1967
- Villordo, O. H., *Genio y figura de E. Mallea*, Beuos Aires 1973
Mansilla, Lucio V.
- 1870 *Una excursión a los indios ranqueles*, Buenos Aires
Mármol, José
- 1851 *Amalia*, Montevideo
- Blasi Brambilla, A., *José Mármol y la sombra de Rosas*, Buenos Aires 1970
Martínez Moreno, Carlos
- 1963 *El paredón*, Barcelona. *The wall*
- 1966 *Con las primeras luces*, Barcelona. *With the first light*
- 1970 *Coca*, Caracas. *Cocaine*
Matto de Turner, Clorinda
- 1889 *Aves sin nido*, Lima, Buenos Aires, Valencia. *Birds without a Nest. A story of Indian life and priestly oppression in Peru*, tr. J. G. Hudson, London 1940. Ed. L. M. Schneider, New York 1968
- Carrillo, Francisco, *Clorinda Matto de Turner y su indigenismo literario*, Lima 1967
Mera, Juan León
- 1879 *Cumandá, o un drama entre salvajes*, Quito; Madrid 1891.
- Sacoto, A., *The Indian in the Ecuadorian Novel*, New York 1967
Onetti, Juan Carlos
- 1939 *El pozo*, Montevideo. 1967 (2nd edition) *The Well*
- 1941 *Tierra de nadie*, Buenos Aires. *No Man's Land*
- 1943 *Para esta noche*, Buenos Aires. *For this night*
- 1950 *La vida breve*, Buenos Aires. *Brief life*
- 1951 *Un sueño realizado y otros cuentos*, Montevideo. *A dream realized and other stories*
- 1954 *Los adioses*, Buenos Aires. *The goodbyes*
- 1959 *Para una tumba sin nombre*, Montevideo. *For a nameless tomb*
- 1960 *La cara de la desgracia*, Montevideo. *The face of misfortune*
- 1961 *Jacob y el otro*, New York. *Jacob and the other man*
- 1961 *El astillero*, Buenos Aires. *The Shipyard*, tr. R. Caffyn, New York 1968
- 1962 *El infierno tan temido*, Montevideo. *Hell so feared*. Short stories
- 1963 *Tan triste como ella*, Montevideo. *As sad as she*
- 1965 *Juntacadáveres*, Montevideo. *Corpsegatherer*
- 1968 *La novia robada y otros cuentos*, Buenos Aires. *The stolen bride and other stories*
- 1973 *La muerte y la niña*, Buenos Aires. *Death and the girl*
- Aínsa, F., *Las trampas de Onetti*, Montevideo 1970
- Giacoman, H. (ed.), *Homenaje a Onetti*, New York 1974
- Rama, A., 'Origen de un novelista y de una generación literaria', in *El pozo*, 1967
Prada, Renato
- 1960 *Los fundadores del alba*, Havana. *The Breach*, tr. W. Redmond, New York 1971
Puig, Manuel
- 1969 *La traición de Rita Hayworth*, Buenos Aires. *Betrayed by Rita Hayworth*, tr. S. J. Levine, New York 1971

- 1970 *Boquitas pintadas*, Buenos Aires. *Heartbreak Tango*, tr. S. J. Levine, New York 1973
- 1973 *The Buenos Aires Affair*, Mexico

Ramos, Graciliano
- 1936 *Angustia*, Rio. *Anguish*, tr. L. C. Kaplan, New York 1946
- 1938 *Vidas secas*, Rio. *Barren Lives*, tr. R. E. Dimmick, Austin 1965
- Feldmann, H., G. Ramos. *Eine Untersuchung zur Selbstdarstellung in seinem epischen Werk*, Geneva–Paris 1965

Rêgo, José Lins do
- 1932 *Meninho do engenho*, Rio. *Plantation Boy* (with Doidinho 1933 and Bangüê 1934), tr. E. Baum, New York 1966

Rivera José Eustacio
- 1924 *La vorágine*, Bogotá. *The Vortex*, tr. E. K. James, New York 1935

Roa Bastos, Augusto
- 1953 *El trueno entre las hojas*, Buenos Aires. *The thunder in the leaves*
- 1959 *Hijo de hombre*, Buenos Aires. *Son of Man*
- 1974 *Yo el supremo*, Buenos Aires
- Foster, D. W., *The Myth of Paraguay in the Fiction of Augusto Roa Bastos*, Chapel Hill 1969
- Giacoman, H. (ed.), *Homenaje a Roa Bastos*, New York 1973

Rosa, João Guimarães
- 1946 *Sagarana*, Rio. Tr. H. de Onis, New York 1966. Short stories
- 1956 *Grande Sertão: Veredas*, Rio. *The Devil to Pay in the Backlands*, tr. J. L. Taylor and H. de Onis, New York 1963
- 1962 *Primeiras estorias*, Rio. *The Third Bank of the River and other stories*, tr. Barbara Shelby, New York 1968

Rulfo, Juan
- 1953 *El llano en llamas*, Mexico. *The Burning Plain*, tr. G. D. Schade, Austin 1968
- 1955 *Pedro Páramo*, Mexico. Tr. L. Kemp, New York 1959
- 1973 *Autobiografía armada*, Buenos Aires 1973
- Rodríguez Alcalá, H., *El arte de Juan Rulfo. Historias de vivos y difuntos*, Mexico 1965
- Sommers, J., *La narrativa de J. Rulfo. Interpretaciones críticas*, Mexico 1974

Sábato, Ernesto
- 1948 *El túnel*, Buenos Aires. *The Outsider*, tr. H. de Onis, New York 1950
- 1961 *Sobre heroes y tumbas*, Buenos Aires
- Giacoman, H. (ed.), *Homenaje a Ernesto Sábato*, New York 1973

Sarmiento, Domingo F.
- 1845 *Facundo. Civilización y barbarie*, Santiago. *Life in the Argentine Republic in the Days of the Tyrants; or, Civilization and Barbarism*, tr. Mrs Horace Mann, New York 1868
- Carilla, E., *Lengua y estilo en Facundo*, Tucuman 1955
- Martínez Estrada, E., *Sarmiento*, Buenos Aires 1946

Vargas Llosa, Mario
- 1959 *Los jefes*, Barcelona. *The chiefs*. Short stories
- 1963 *La ciudad y los perros*, Barcelona. *The Time of the Hero*, tr. L. Kemp, London 1966
- 1966 *La casa verde*, Barcelona. *The Green House*, tr. G. Rabassa New York 1969
- 1967 *Los cachorros. Pichula Cuellar*, Barcelona. *The cubs*

- 1969 *Conversación en la Catedral*, Barcelona, 2 vols. *Conversation in The Cathedral*, tr. G. Rabassa, New York 1975
- 1973 *Pantaleón y las visitadoras*, Barcelona. *Pantaleon and the Whores*
- Alonso, M. R., *Agresión a la realidad. Mario Vargas Llosa*, Las Palmas 1971
- Boldori, R., *Maria Vargas Llosa y la literatura en el Perú de hoy*, Santa Fe, Argentina, 1969
- Diez, L. A., *Mario Vargas Llosa's pursuit of the total novel*, Mexico 1970.
- Giacoman, H. (ed.), *Homenaje a Vargas Llosa*, New York 1972
- Oviedo, J. M., *Mario Vargas Llosa. La invención de una realidad*, Barcelona 1970
- Vargas Llosa, M., *Historia secreta de una novela*, Barcelona 1971

Viñas, David
- 1967 *Los hombres de a caballo*, Havana

Yáñez, Agustín
- 1955 *Al filo del agua*, Mexico. *The Edge of the Storm*, tr. Ethel Brinton, Austin 1963
- 1962 *Las tierras flacas*, Mexico. *The Lean Lands*, tr. Ethel Brinton, Austin 1968
- Giacoman, H. (ed.), *Homenaje a Agustín Yáñez*, New York 1973

INDEX

Italic figures indicate major references

Acevedo Díaz, Eduardo, 142
Agustín, José, 139
Aínsa, Fernando, 145
Alegría, Ciro, 21, 54, 104, 147
Alencar, José de, 18
Altamirano, Ignacio, 18–19, 76, 143
Alvarado, Pedro de, 34
Amadis, 138
Amado, Jorge, 142
Andes, 3, 17, 20, 21, 102–4, 106, 108, 117
Antonioni, Michelangelo, 146
Arbenz, Jacobo, 35, 144
Arenas, Reinaldo, 3, 149
Argentina, 11, 14, 34, 85, 87, 89
Arguedas, Alcides, 17, 20–1, 30, 104, 143
Arguedas, José María, 1, 3, 4, 12, 17, 21, 39, *98–109*, 117, 133, 135, 137, 139, 140, 147; *The Fox from Above and the Fox from Below*, 1, *98–109*, 140; *The Deep Rivers*, 39, 105, 106; *Every Blood*, 39, 105, 107; *El Sexto*, 104; *Yawar Fiesta*, 104
Arlt, Roberto, 145
Artaud, Antonin, 78
Asturias, Miguel Ángel, 1, 13, 15, 21, 22, 23, *25–44*, 51, 58, 69, 75, 103, 108, 120, 135, 136, 137, 140, 143–4, 149; *Men of Maize*, 15, *25–44*, 136; *The Social Problem of the Indian*, 30, 31; *Legends of Guatemala*, 31, 35, 51; *The President*, 35, *40–4*, 120; 'Banana Trilology', 35; *Strong Wind*, 35, 135; *Weekend in Guatemala*, 35; *Three of the Four Suns*, 35; *The*

Mulatto and Mr Fly, 36, 37, 44; *Maladron*, 36, 37, 44
Aztec, 18, 19, 22, 143, 148
Azuela, Mariano, 77, 78, 146

Balzac, Honoré de, 8, 9, 22, 148
barbarism, 5, 7, 8, 13
Barrios, Eduardo, 3
Bello, Andrés, 8, 16, 18
Benedetti, Mario, 2, 145
Bible, 32, 53, 127
Black Culture, 50, 51, 52, 54, 57, 126, 129
Blest Gana, Alberto, 8–12
Bolivia, 2
Borges, Jorge Luis, 3, 10, 11, 22–24, 69, 85, 93, 135, 139; *Fictions* 22–4, 93
Bourgeoisie, 5, 9–13, 18, 19, 29, 43, 47, 118, 120, 127, 128, 136
Bourget, Paul, 11
Brazil, 1, 2, 7, 18, 77, 95, 142, *see also* sertão
Brazilian Americanists, 18, 19, 140
Breton, André, 43, 51
Buenos Aires, 5, 8, 11, 12, 14, 64, 65, 66, 83, 85, 86, 92
Butor, Michel, 143

Cabrera Infante, Guillermo, 2
Cakchiquels, *Annals* of, 22, 30–3, 143
Cambaceres, Eugenio, 11–12, 89
Cardenal, Ernesto, 39, 141, 144
Cardoso, Onelio Jorge, 2
Caribbean, 4, 47–9, 55, 57, 58, 124, 137, 149
Carpentier, Alejo, 1, 2, 13, 15, 16, 22, 37, *45–59*, 65, 69, 100, 101, 102, 124, 125, 130, 133, 136–7, 141, 144–5, 149; *The Lost Steps,*